Math on Call

Teacher's Resource Book

Virginia H. Sullaway

Nancy E. Wilson

GReaT SouRCe®
EDUCATION GROUP
A Houghton Mifflin Company
New Ways to Know®

Ginny Sullaway is currently a Mathematics Specialist at Olle Middle School in the Alief Independent School District, Alief, Texas. All of her instructional experience is at the middle school level.

Nancy E. Wilson is currently a Mathematics Specialist at O'Donnell Middle School in the Alief Independent School District, Alief, Texas. She has taught middle school students for over 20 years.

Credits:
Design and Production: PC&F, Inc.

Illustration Credits:
Robot Characters: Inkwell Studios
Creative Art: Joe Spooner
Technical Art: PC&F, Inc.

Printed in the United States of America
Great Source and *New Ways to Know* are registered trademarks of Houghton Mifflin Company.
International Standard Book Number: 0-669-46923-8
    4 5 6 7 8 9 10 MZ 04 03 02 01
URL address: http://www.greatsource.com/

Table of Contents

Numeration

Number Theory

Computation

Algebra

Graphs and Statistics

Geometry

Ratio, Proportion, and Percent

Probability and Odds

Copymasters

▶ Uses for the Math on Call Handbook

Math on Call is intended as a reference handbook for students, teachers, and parents. It provides concise explanations and examples that are written on the student level. *Math on Call*, with instructional support from teachers, is a tool that can empower students to become more responsible for their own learning, reviewing, relearning, research, and extended thinking.

Middle-school students frequently ask, "Why do I have to learn this?" They want to be actively involved moving, socializing, measuring, and doing mathematics. Often the middle-school classroom can contain a wide variety of abilities as well as a wide variety of learning styles. The handbook and the activities in the teacher's resource book have been written with the middle-school student in mind. The activities provide rich in-depth views of some topics and quick applications for others.

TEACHER USES

The *Math on Call* handbook is an excellent teacher reference for unique facts and examples of particular relationships that are explained in a higher-level text. For example, domain and range are normally studied in-depth in first year algebra. A sixth-grade teacher might not find the explanation in his or her text, but can begin to use the vocabulary and concepts in an informal approach that will give younger students a richer background.

Math on Call contains definitions and explanations that are easy to communicate to students. For example, item number 426 gives an excellent explanation of the difference between fractions and ratios.

Math on Call is organized by topics, not by chapters. Some students may be ready to review addition with all types of rational numbers. Others may need a quick review of addition of whole numbers. *Math on Call* brings all those skills together in one section.

Teachers in other disciplines who don't normally teach mathematics will also find *Math on Call* to be a handy reference. Social studies teachers often teach concepts of graphs, charts and statistics. Yet they may need some specific background information about individual types of graphs, or measures of central tendencies. For science teachers, the information about extrapolation and interpolation with graphs found in item numbers 311 and 312 can help them better instruct students in the prediction of events not specifically measured. Language arts teachers may refer to the book for writing activities, vocabulary building, and for finding appropriate connections to language development.

Vocabulary is an area of mathematics that is often overlooked or not emphasized. *Math on Call* provides an avenue for a stronger approach to terms and their applications. The use of vocabulary in instruction also provides ways for students who have difficulty with computation to excel through their understanding of verbal relationships and meanings.

STUDENT USES

The language of mathematics is a stumbling block for many students. The use of mathematically correct vocabulary along with the examples helps students to connect words with symbols. The glossary provides a comprehensive resource of math terms.

Student research is an important part of middle-school education. Students can readily find examples and related topics by following the "More Help" references in the book. The book offers many examples, and there are direct links between computational skills and their applications in a real-world context.

Math on Call can be a handy reference for students completing makeup work or homework assignments. There are times when explanations in the regular textbook need further clarification. *Math on Call* gives new explanations that allow students to understand a difficult topic more fully. The pictures, charts, and simple explanations fill gaps in learning that a student may have, but is unlikely to voice.

Math on Call is also an economical handbook and reference when no textbook is available. Teachers may choose not to use textbooks for a variety of reasons. *Math on Call* provides a ready reference for students whose notes are incomplete or indecipherable when they are doing homework on their own.

PARENT USES

Math on Call is a concise handbook of middle-school math topics that parents can readily use. Math textbooks often have a detailed explanation of a single skill. *Math on Call* presents those single skills in a larger context and connects concepts to previous learning. Many parents may find this a useful mechanism for recalling mathematical steps that have grown rusty over time, enabling them to remember the sequence of steps to write fractions with common denominators, for example. *Math on Call* shows these steps with diagrams, words, and models.

Today, students are approaching mathematics topics with many more manipulatives than were used in previous generations. The advent of the calculator has also changed the nature of mathematical instruction. One example of the support *Math on Call* provides is in item number 210, where parents are offered a way to determine if the calculator their child is using follows the rules for order of operations.

The wide variety of diagrams and clear explanations in *Math on Call* give parents a great resource to help with homework. Equipping parents to help improve their child's learning is a benefit that reaches far beyond the classroom.

How to Use This Teacher's Resource Book

The organization of this book parallels the sections of *Math on Call.* You may want to first correlate the chapters of your textbook to the sections of *Math on Call.* This will enable a ready reference to the activities in this book. A listing of the sections of *Math on Call* is provided below. Each section may include more than one chapter of your text.

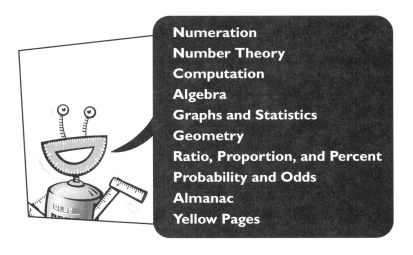

Numeration
Number Theory
Computation
Algebra
Graphs and Statistics
Geometry
Ratio, Proportion, and Percent
Probability and Odds
Almanac
Yellow Pages

Math on Call Teacher's Resource Book is intended to provide classroom assignments on topics that may be new for many students. Intentionally, no grade levels are assigned to the activities. For some students the problem may be an investigation to extend known topics. For example, a student who understands area of circles and squares can view "Hats Off to the Chef" as an open-ended problem with no specific answer. Some activities, such as "Susan Selects Sully Soda," can be used as a direct application of a lesson on unit prices and comparing decimals. The activities are designed to connect many of those topics that relate to more than one area of mathematics, such as geometry and number theory.

Some activities are explorations to investigate special or unique relationships, such as the Golden Ratio. Other activities, such as "High Guy," provide teachers the steps to complete a problem often pictured on standardized tests, but less often actually researched and computed.

These activities are also designed to provide examples of mathematics as it relates to jobs and professions, and daily tasks such as shopping or playing. Most activities have extensions listed on the teacher page so that students may continue studies on the topic. Many of the extensions provide more in-depth study and may serve as springboards for math fairs and projects.

Also in this book is a rubric that you may use for grading many of the activities.

General Marshall's Survey

30 minutes

OBJECTIVE

- Explore the *Math on Call* handbook to determine the format of the book

MATERIALS

- *Math on Call* handbook

TEACHER NOTES

- This activity leads students on a tour through the *Math on Call* handbook and enables them to become more familiar with the structure of the book. It also prepares them for the structure of the activities in this book.

- Have students correlate chapters of their textbook to the sections of *Math on Call*. Often more than one chapter may relate to a section of the book.

ANSWERS

1. 11 including the index

2. Each section has its own color.

3. Definitions, procedures, explanations, and rules are given as examples of things that might be looked up in *Math on Call*.

4. Because there may be more than one topic on a page

5. Any 3 of the 10 sub-sections listed in item number 473 would be acceptable answers.

6. In "How to Use This Book," page ix, the index, glossary, and table of contents are listed as places to begin looking for information.

7. Yellow. The purpose is to call attention to possible errors or misunderstandings.

8. Item number 476 in the Almanac. Problem-Solving Strategies and Problem-Solving Skills.

9. A computer can be used for spreadsheets, databases, and the Internet.

10. $47 + 8 = 55$.

11. A parallelepiped is a prism whose bases and faces are all parallelograms.

12. Extrapolation predicts a value from information not on a graph. Interpolation predicts a value between data points on a graph.

13. The mean, median, and mode are three types of average.

14. A perfect number is a number equal to the sum of its factors, not including the number itself. A perfect square is the product of an integer multiplied by itself.

15. Precision is an indication of how finely a measurement is made. Money is represented to the hundredths place, so the precision of an answer can be measured to the same place.

16. Answers will vary. An equation shows that two mathematical expressions are equal.

17.

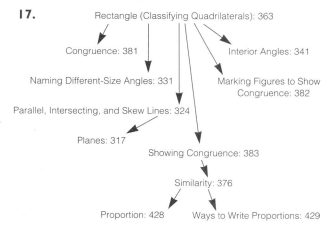

Rectangle (Classifying Quadrilaterals): 363

Congruence: 381

Interior Angles: 341

Naming Different-Size Angles: 331

Marking Figures to Show Congruence: 382

Parallel, Intersecting, and Skew Lines: 324

Planes: 317

Showing Congruence: 383

Similarity: 376

Proportion: 428

Ways to Write Proportions: 429

▶ General Marshall's Survey

A General determines the lay of the land before designing a plan of attack. This lesson is to let you determine the lay of the land in the *Math on Call* handbook.

This spot will normally give you key references. This lesson is to familiarize you with the format of *Math on Call*.

References to MATH ON CALL

1. How many sections are there in *Math on Call*? _____

2. How can you tell one section from another section?

   _____

3. Find page vi, "How This Book Is Organized." What four things might you look up in this book?

   _____

4. Why do you think the topics are numbered, rather than the pages?

   _____

5. List three things that you will use in the Almanac.

   _____

6. List the three places to begin looking for information.

   _____

7. Look for a Math Alert box in each section. What color are they?

   _____ What is the purpose of the Math Alert?

   _____

8. *Math on Call* has some guidelines for problem solving. Where are they found?

   _____

   What are the two sub-sections of the Problem Solving section?

   _____

9. *Math on Call* lists three ways that a computer can be used for math. What are they?

   _____

General Marshall's Survey, cont.

Now let's use *Math on Call* as a reference book.

10. Write the sum of the 15th prime number plus the perfect cube of 2.

_____

11. What is a parallelepiped? _____

12. What is the difference between extrapolation and interpolation?

_____

13. What are three types of average? _____

14. How are a perfect number and a perfect square different?

_____

15. What is precision? _____

How precise can your answer be if the problem is $21.65 ÷ 2$?

_____

16. The terms *equation* and *expression* are commonly used in math. Study the Yellow Pages definitions of these words and write an example of each one. Then explain your thinking.

Equation _____   Expression _____

17. For many topics in *Math on Call* there are "More Help" messages. These messages refer you to related topics. For example:

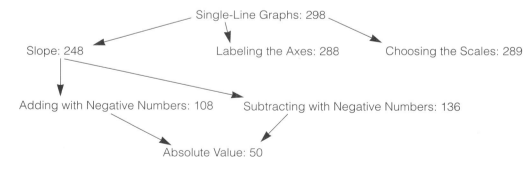

Start with the word *rectangle* from the Yellow Pages. On the back of this page, draw the network of resources that you would follow to find every piece of information possible. For each branch, write the topic title and item number.

Rectangle: 363

Under Construction

OBJECTIVE

• Understand compass constructions to create specific angles

MATERIALS

• compass
• straightedge
• additional paper

TEACHER NOTES

• Compass constructions provide an opportunity to review basic vocabulary and definitions, such as point, line, arc, intersection, and so on.

• Allow time for students to practice using a compass and straightedge until they are comfortable. Making decorative pictures is a good way to practice. Encourage students to make large constructions initially. Note that students with fine-motor-coordination difficulties may proceed more slowly than other students.

EXTENSIONS

• Students can experiment to see which regular polygons can be inscribed in a circle using compass constructions.

• Have students research the construction of a regular pentagon.

• Have students explore computer programs designed to create geometric constructions.

ANSWERS

1. Rulers have measurement marks; straightedges do not.

2. Answers will vary, but may include books, folders, notebooks, and so on.

3. It is a line that divides a line segment in half and meets the segment at right angles.

4. Draw a line segment, construct a perpendicular bisector, and label the angle.

5. It is a line passing through the vertex of an angle, dividing it into 2 congruent angles.

6. Construct a 90° angle, then construct an angle bisector, and label each 45° angle.

7. Note that 135° = 90° + 45°. Construct two adjacent 90° angles. Bisect one of the angles. Label 135° using the full 90° angle and the resulting adjacent 45° angle.

8. All its angles are 60°.

9. Construct an equilateral triangle, bisect one angle, and label the 30° angle.

10. Note that 105° = 60° + 45°. Construct an equilateral triangle. Construct a 45° angle. Copy the 45° angle so it is adjacent to one of the 60° angles of the triangle. Label the 105° angle.

11–14. Check all student compass constructions to make sure students understand the concepts and procedures involved.

▶ Under Construction

The Ancient Greeks were the first to explore compass constructions. Pretend you are a student of Euclid, and you have only a compass and straightedge to do your constructions.

After you have practiced the basic constructions, complete these questions using the information in *Math on Call*. Do the constructions on the back of this page or on another sheet of paper.

Angle Bisectors: **336**

Angles Formed by Lines Cut by a Transversal: **338**

Central Angles: **340**

Congruence: **381**

Geometric Constructions: **512–523**

References to MATH ON CALL

I. How is a straightedge different from a ruler? _____

_____

2. Name three things in your classroom you could use as a straightedge.

_____   _____   _____

3. What is a perpendicular bisector? _____

4. Tell how you would construct a 90° angle. _____

_____

Construct a 90° angle.

5. What is an angle bisector? _____

6. Tell how you would construct a 45° angle. _____

_____

Construct a 45° angle.

7. Tell how you would construct a 135° angle. _____

_____

Construct a 135° angle.

8. What do you know about the angles of an equilateral triangle? _____

_____

9. Tell how you would construct a 30° angle. _____

_____

Construct a 30° angle.

10. Tell how you would construct a 105° angle. _____

_____

Construct a 105° angle.

▶ Under Construction, cont.

"Excellent!" praised Euclid. "Now complete these constructions on your wax tablets." Use another sheet of paper for these constructions.

Inscribing a polygon in a circle means drawing a polygon whose vertices are on the circle.

11. Follow these directions to inscribe a hexagon in a circle.

    a. Draw a circle. Keep your compass setting the same.

    b. Place the point of your compass anywhere on the circle. Make a mark on the circle. Move the compass to that mark and make another mark. Continue around the circle until you have made 6 marks.

    c. Draw a line segment from each mark to the next mark in order.

For fun, place the point of your compass on one of the marks and draw an arc connecting the 2 marks on either side of the point. If you repeat this procedure at each mark, you create a "compass flower."

12. Follow these directions to inscribe an equilateral triangle in a circle.

    a. Follow steps (a) and (b) above.

    b. Draw line segments, connecting every other mark.

13. Follow these directions to inscribe a 6-pointed star in a circle.

    a. Repeat the procedure for inscribing an equilateral triangle in a circle.

    b. Draw line segments, connecting the remaining marks on the circle.

14. Develop a procedure to construct a congruent triangle by the Angle-Side-Angle method. This means you should copy two angles and the side between them. Experiment with the triangle below.

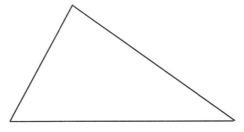

Draw another triangle. Have a friend use your triangle to try out the procedure. Test for congruence by placing your triangle directly on top of the copy. It should fit perfectly.

► Assessment: "Is This for a Grade?"

Many of the activities in this book are open-ended and have more than one solution. Sometimes the processes used to solve these problems are more important than the answers themselves. Process thinking and communication skills are as key to the educational process as computation and correctness. Too many times children erase experimental work and computational mistakes. "Rough drafts," common in language arts classes, need to be encouraged in the math class in order to see how students process the problem.

Open-ended questions can challenge traditional grading systems. Students and teachers need to spend more time communicating to ensure a rich mathematical experience. Richer problems require a broader type of assessment for both teacher and student. The rubrics that follow were designed for this reason. Students may be able to compute an answer yet have no clear understanding of the concepts behind the answer, or how it relates to other areas of mathematical thinking. The rubric allows for assessment in different areas and at different levels.

The rubrics are designed to evaluate five areas. The five areas are comprehension, application and analysis, mechanics, presentation, and aesthetics. Students must be able to identify the problem, develop and execute a plan, obtain an answer, communicate and present that answer, and do all this in a way that encourages pride and positive comments. The medals were chosen to mark degrees of skill for each of these areas, and to give vocabulary to make communication easier.

The teacher rubric gives descriptions of expectations. While it is the goal that every child attain the gold level in every area, the truth is that student work may be gold in one area and bronze in another. The rubric is intended to be broad enough to evaluate work on several levels. More students may experience success due to the five areas of assessment.

The rubric also provides a method for teachers to communicate their expectations to students and parents. Open-ended problems can be so broad that some students are not sure where to begin. The rubric gives the teacher a way to help students begin looking for facts and developing a plan, then moving on to a solution.

If teachers need to place a grade on a project, then each cell can be given a value and a total numerical grade can be created. Every product need not be evaluated in this way. A holistic grade can also be determined by a teacher.

The use of student rubrics is a method to improve process thinking while students assess their own work and that of others. The peer and student rubrics are written in "kid terms." They are not intended to be used without discussion of the expectations stated on the teacher rubric. Student self-assessment and peer assessment are excellent ways to share ideas, develop communication skills, and allow each child to share his or her strengths.

Copymasters for the teacher, student, and peer rubrics appear on the following three pages.

Teacher Assessment Rubric

Name _____

	Gold	Silver	Bronze	Copper
Comprehension	Specific facts and relationships are identified and well-defined.	Most facts and relationships are defined.	Some facts are identified but relationships are missing.	No facts or relationships stated.
Application and Analysis	A strong plan is developed and executed correctly.	A plan is developed and implemented with some computational errors.	Some organized computation toward a weak plan.	Random computation with little relation to problem. No plan is present.
Mechanics	Appropriate and correct computation, mathematical representations, and graphics.	Appropriate computation that may be incorrect. Mathematical representation and graphics are present.	Computation is wrong and leads to further mistakes.	Computation is random. Mathematical representations are non-existent.
Presentation	Strong and succinct communication of results.	Strong communication of results. Justification for method may be weak.	Communication of results is present, but lacks any justification.	No results are communicated. No justification is to be found. A correct answer may have appeared.
Aesthetics	Exceptional. Attractive. Encourages attention. All requirements exceeded.	Neat and orderly. Requirements met.	Messy and disorganized. Requirements missing.	Illegible and random information. Most requirements missing.

►Student Self-Assessment Rubric

Name _____

	Gold	Silver	Bronze	Copper
Do I know what to do?	I used the right numbers and the right plan.	I used some right numbers and an OK plan.	I used some right numbers but I need a plan.	I haven't got a clue.
Can I do it?	I got it all done and can defend my answer(s).	I got it all done and most of it is right.	I got some of it done and I think it's right.	I got some answers but I'm not sure they're right.
Is it right?	There are no mistakes. I think my pictures are great.	Oops! I made a couple of careless errors.	I made mistakes that messed up the other answers.	I can't tell if it's right.
Is my work clear?	Everyone could understand my work.	I may need to explain some of my work.	I'll definitely need to explain my work.	I hope no one asks me about my work.
How does it look?	Wow! Maybe I can help somebody else next time!	It could have been neater.	This looks really unorganized.	I should have asked for help.

Peer Assessment Rubric

Name _____

	Gold	Silver	Bronze	Copper
Do you know what to do?	You used the right numbers and the right plan.	You used some right numbers and an OK plan.	You used some right numbers but you need a plan.	You may not have a clue.
Can you do it?	You got it all done perfectly.	You got it all done and most of it is right.	You got some answers but your plan has some holes.	You got several answers but I don't see a clear plan here.
Is it right?	There are no mistakes. Your pictures are great.	Oops! You made a couple of careless errors.	You made some mistakes that messed up the other answers.	You're on the wrong track.
Is the work clear?	Everyone could understand your work.	You may need to explain some of your work.	You'll definitely need to explain your work.	I hope no one asks you about your work.
How does it look?	Wow! Can you help me next time?	It could have been neater.	You need help organizing your work.	You should have asked for help.

Who's on First?

30-45 minutes

OBJECTIVES

- Compare and order decimals
- Understand place value of decimals
- Determine from real-world examples whether the largest decimal number is better or not

MATERIALS

- sports almanac (optional)

TEACHER NOTES

- This activity is intended to provide a real-world example of comparing decimals. Before doing this activity, select some decimal numbers and have students practice putting them in order.

- Have students identify different games or sports and determine in each case if a high score is better than a low score. Golf, soccer, track and field events, and basketball are good examples to consider.

- Distribute copies of the student page. Have students determine which person and number goes with which category in the first table. Have them fill in the table.

- Students should now decide what is a winning number in each category (high or low), and place the names and numbers in order in the second table.

- Have students write a few sentences to justify the order they have chosen.

EXTENSIONS

- Have students decide on a real-world situation involving decimals and write their own scenario. Comparing prices of items in food or department stores might be a good place to begin. Changes in the prices of shares of stock on the stock market could provide another scenario.

- Investigate other sports and determine how to compare athletes through the use of statistics.

- Two of the players listed on the chart held the NBA Scoring Leader title for 7 consecutive years. Which two are they? How would you find out? (The players are Wilt Chamberlain, who held the title from 1960 to 1966, and Michael Jordan, who held it from 1987 to 1993. Suggest a sports almanac or the Internet as ways to find the information.)

ANSWERS

Batting Average— greatest average number of hits		Earned Run Average (ERA)—lowest number of runs earned by opponents		NBA Average Points per Game—highest average points scored per game		Women's 200m Freestyle—fastest time	
Babe Ruth	0.378	Kevin Brown	1.89	Wilt Chamberlain	50.4	Heike Friedrick	1:57.65
Willie Mays	0.345	Greg Maddux	2.72	Michael Jordan	37.1	Nicole Haislett	1:57.90
Jackie Robinson	0.342	Hideo Nomo	3.19	Kareem Abdul-Jabbar	34.8	Barbara Krause	1:58.33
Hank Aaron	0.328	Pat Hentgen	3.22	David Robinson	29.8	Mary Wayle	1:59.23

Source: *Information Please Almanac*

Numeration

▶ Who's on First?

Decimals: Place Value: 012

Equivalent Decimals: 017

Comparing Decimals:
   018, 019

Ordering Decimals: 020

**References to
MATH ON CALL**

Imagine going through time, selecting various athletes, and trying to determine who was the best. Listed below are athletes and their statistics. For the first chart, your job is to classify the athletes. The second chart should then be completed with the best statistic first.

Michael Jordan	37.1	Heike Friedrick	1:57.65
Babe Ruth	0.378	David Robinson	29.8
Greg Maddux	2.72	Hideo Nomo	3.19
Kareem Abdul-Jabbar	34.8	Jackie Robinson	0.342
Mary Wayle	1:59.23	Nicole Haislett	1:57.90
Hank Aaron	0.328	Willie Mays	0.345
Kevin Brown	1.89	Pat Hentgen	3.22
Barbara Krause	1:58.33	Wilt Chamberlain	50.4

1. Fill in the tables. Categorize the people and statistics first.

Batting Average	Earned Run Average (ERA)*	NBA Average Points per Game	200m Freestyle

*(The ERA is the average number of earned runs against a pitcher per 9 innings pitched.)

2. Now put the people in order starting with the best score in each category.

Batting Average	Earned Run Average (ERA)	NBA Average Points per Game	200m Freestyle

3. Tell how you determined the order for each group. _____

_____

_____

_____

Susan Selects Sully Soda

OBJECTIVES

- Compare and order decimals
- Compare unit pricing of products to determine the best buy

MATERIALS

- calculators

30–45 minutes

TEACHER NOTES

- Remind students that the total number of fluid ounces must be determined for each package.
- Make sure students understand what the unit of each package is. The 6 and 12 packs of cans have units of 12 fluid ounces each, while the 6 pack of bottles has a unit of 20 fluid ounces. The 2-liter bottle is one unit by itself; students do not need to multiply by 2 to find the total fluid ounces in this package.
- The cost per ounce may give some students a little trouble. One way to remember what to do is to read "cost per ounce" as a mathematical sentence. Put a division symbol in place of the "per," and read it as "the total cost ÷ the total number of ounces."

EXTENSIONS

- Have students compare these prices to those in a local store. How close are they? How do different brands compare? How do "sale" prices compare to "regular" prices?

2. The least expensive package of Sully Soda is the 2-liter bottle.

3. From lowest to highest cost per fluid ounce the order is:

2-liter bottle

12 pack of cans

6 pack of bottles

6 pack of cans

4. Answers will vary. Students might say that they would buy a 6 pack to ensure that everyone gets the same amount to drink, no matter what the cost. Others might buy the 12 pack to provide enough for the class and leave the 6 extras at home. Still others may point out that buying the 2-liter bottle means that cups also need to be purchased, raising another question about comparison shopping.

ANSWERS

1.

Sully Soda	fl oz per unit	total fl oz	cost	cost per fl oz
6 pack of cans	12 fl oz	72 fl oz	$1.49	$0.02069
12 pack of cans	12 fl oz	144 fl oz	$2.49	$0.01729
6 pack of bottles	20 fl oz	120 fl oz	$2.39	$0.01991
2-liter bottle	67.6 fl oz	67.6 fl oz	$1.09	$0.01612

Numeration

▶ Susan Selects Sully Soda

Susan sits in Mrs. Gideon's Language Arts class. The class is having a party to celebrate everyone passing a test. Each person needs to bring something. Four people will bring soda for the class of 23. Mrs. Gideon has asked Susan to bring soda for 6 people. Help Susan make the best selection.

Decimals: Place Value: **012**

Equivalent Decimals: **017**

Comparing Decimals: **018**

Ordering Decimals: **020**

Rate: **435**

Unit Price: **438**

Comparing Unit Prices to Find the Better Buy: **439**

References to MATH ON CALL

12 pack
12 fl oz/can
$2.49

6 pack
12 fl oz/can
$1.49

12 12-oz.
cans

6 pack
20 fl oz/bottle
$2.39

2-liter
bottle (67.6 fl oz) $1.09

1. Complete the table. Compute the cost per fluid ounce for each of the different packages of Sully Soda.

Sully Soda	fl oz per unit	total fl oz	cost	cost per fl oz
6 pack of cans	12 fl oz	72 fl oz	$1.49	$0.02069
12 pack of cans				
6 pack of bottles				
2-liter bottle				

2. Which package has the lowest cost per fluid ounce? _____

3. List the different packages in order from the lowest cost per fluid ounce to the highest cost per fluid ounce.

_____

_____

_____

_____

4. Which package would you buy for your class party? _____

Why? _____

_____

_____

Numeration

"Doctor, Is It Terminal?"

OBJECTIVE

- Identify a pattern in the prime factorization of the denominators of fractions that represents repeating or terminating decimals

MATERIALS

- calculators
- Math Notebook Page, page 119

TEACHER NOTES

- Discuss with students how fractions with the same factor in both the numerator and the denominator can be simplified by removing fractions equaling 1. For example, $2 \div 2 = 1$.

- You may want to have students work in small groups to answer questions 14 and 15. Sometimes it is easier to talk about discovering patterns than trying to write it all down. If you want to provide a hint, direct students to look for the common factors in the denominators of the "non-repeating" fractions.

EXTENSIONS

- Students can write a note to a friend in another class about their discovery.

- Examine the "non-repeaters" with the students. Since these fractions have prime factors in the denominator of only 2 and/or 5, ask students to think about how this contributes to our decimal system. How might the fact that we have two hands with five fingers on each hand relate to this?

- Have students create two 3-digit denominators that will be "terminators" when written as decimals. Will different numerators with these "terminator" denominators make a difference?

ANSWERS

1. $0.3\overline{5}$

2. $0.\overline{428571}$

3. $0.4\overline{5}$

4. $0.4\overline{5}$

5. $0.41\overline{6}$

6. 0.4

7. 0.45

8. 0.25

9. 0.85

10. 0.475

11. A "repeater" is a fraction that, when written as a decimal, has an infinitely repeating pattern of digits.

12. A "non-repeater" is a fraction that, when written as a decimal, has a definite end to the digits.

13. A better word for "non-repeater" is "terminator."

14. When a "non-repeater" is written in simplest form, the prime factorization of the denominator contains only twos and fives.

15. When a fraction is written in simplest form, if the prime factorization of the denominator contains any factor other than 2 or 5, the fraction is a "repeater." If the factors in the denominator are only 2 and/or 5, then the fraction is a "non-repeater."

▶ "Doctor, Is It Terminal?"

Use *Math on Call* and a calculator to determine the decimal equivalent of the fractions in both boxes below.

**References to
MATH ON CALL**

"Repeaters"

1. $\frac{16}{45}$ = _____   2. $\frac{27}{63}$ = _____   3. $\frac{55}{121}$ = _____

4. $\frac{35}{77}$ = _____   5. $\frac{5}{12}$ = _____

"Non-repeaters"

6. $\frac{14}{35}$ = _____   7. $\frac{18}{40}$ = _____   8. $\frac{29}{116}$ = _____

9. $\frac{17}{20}$ = _____   10. $\frac{57}{120}$ = _____

11. What is your definition of a "repeater"? _____
_____

12. What is your definition of a "non-repeater"? _____
_____

13. What might be a better word for the "non-repeater" group?
_____

These are "repeaters."

$\frac{16}{45}$ **27** / **63** $\frac{5}{12}$ $\frac{35}{77}$ $\frac{55}{121}$

On your Math Notebook Page, write the prime factorization of the numerator and denominator for the fractions in both boxes.

For example, $\frac{8}{30} = \frac{2 \times 2 \times 2}{2 \times 3 \times 5}$.

Then write each fraction in its simplest form.

For example, $\frac{2 \times 2 \times 2}{2 \times 3 \times 5} = \frac{2 \times 2}{3 \times 5} = \frac{4}{15}$.

14. What do you notice? _____
_____

15. Does the prime factorization of the denominator provide any clues for your earlier definitions of "repeaters" and "non-repeaters"?
_____
_____

These are "non-repeaters."

$\frac{14}{35}$ $\frac{29}{116}$ $\frac{18}{40}$ $\frac{57}{120}$ $\frac{17}{20}$

Numeration

On Your Mark . . .

30–45 minutes

OBJECTIVES

- Define benchmark fractions
- Estimate equivalent fractions, decimals, and percents
- Compare and order fractions, decimals, and percents

MATERIALS

- calculators (optional)

TEACHER NOTES

- This activity allows students to develop an understanding of the size of fractions, decimals, and percents. It also helps students connect the equivalent values of fractions, decimals, and percents.

- Estimating fractions, decimals, and percents is very difficult. This activity might be used early in the year so that ongoing review can occur. You may want to post the table from question 2 on the classroom wall. This will provide a reference for students.

EXTENSIONS

- To provide practice in computation with fractions, have students create 2 fractions by rolling a 1–6 number cube 4 times. Placement of the digits within the fractions will be determined by the operation (addition, subtraction, multiplication, or division) you choose to use. The answer in each case should yield a result as close to 1 as possible. Try a few examples with the students first to make sure they understand the size of fractions and what will happen given the specific operation.

- Use newspaper advertisements and benchmark fractions to estimate sale prices in local stores.

ANSWERS

1. In item number 032, *Math on Call* defines benchmark fractions as fractions that are used *a lot* and are helpful in picturing other fractions.

2. Listed below are all the equivalencies.

3. $\frac{39}{63} \approx \frac{40}{60} = \frac{2}{3}$

$\frac{42}{51} \approx \frac{40}{50} = \frac{4}{5}$

$\frac{11}{96} \approx \frac{10}{100} = \frac{1}{10}$

$\frac{21}{38} \approx \frac{20}{40} = \frac{1}{2}$

4. $32\% \approx 33\% \approx \frac{1}{3}$

$72\% \approx 75\% = \frac{3}{4}$

$99.4\% \approx 100\% = \frac{1}{1}$

$9\% \approx 10\% = \frac{1}{10}$

$48\% \approx 50\% = \frac{1}{2}$

5. $0.12 = \frac{12}{100} \approx \frac{10}{100} = \frac{1}{10}$

$0.36 = \frac{36}{100} \approx \frac{40}{100} = \frac{2}{5}$

$0.453 = \frac{453}{1000} \approx \frac{500}{1000} = \frac{1}{2}$

$0.785 = \frac{785}{1000} \approx \frac{800}{1000} = \frac{4}{5}$

$1.007 = \frac{1007}{1000} \approx \frac{1000}{1000} = \frac{1}{1}$

fraction	$\frac{1}{10}$	$\frac{1}{4}$	$\frac{1}{3}$	$\frac{2}{5}$	$\frac{1}{2}$	$\frac{2}{3}$	$\frac{3}{4}$	$\frac{4}{5}$	$\frac{9}{10}$	$\frac{1}{1}$
decimal	0.1	0.25	$0.\overline{3}$	0.4	0.5	$0.\overline{6}$	0.75	0.8	0.9	1.0
percent	10%	25%	$33\frac{1}{3}\%$	40%	50%	$66\frac{2}{3}\%$	75%	80%	90%	100%

▶ On Your Mark . . .

**References to
MATH ON CALL**

A **benchmark** is known as a standard for measurement. In the past, artisans often made marks in their wooden work benches to indicate measurements they used often. This saved them from having to remeasure every time. Today, surveyors use benchmarks to set reference points on known heights. Mathematicians use benchmarks to identify critical numbers.

1. How does *Math on Call* define benchmark fractions?

_____

_____

2. In the table below, a common fraction, decimal, or percent that is a handy benchmark appears in each column. Complete the table by writing the missing equivalent fraction, decimal, or percent in each column.

fraction	$\frac{1}{10}$			$\frac{2}{5}$			$\frac{3}{4}$			$\frac{1}{1}$
decimal		0.25				$0.\overline{6}$		0.8		
percent			$33\frac{1}{3}\%$		50%				90%	

3. To use benchmark fractions, you may want to round the numerator and denominator of a fraction to be near a known benchmark fraction. Round each of these fractions, and write the benchmark it is near.

$\frac{39}{63}$ _____ $\frac{42}{51}$ _____

$\frac{11}{96}$ _____ $\frac{21}{38}$ _____

4. To determine the benchmark fraction nearest to these percents, round the percents and then pick the appropriate fraction to match.

32% _____   72% _____   99.4% _____

9% _____   48% _____

5. Decimals can be estimated using benchmarks fractions. Rename each of these decimals as a fraction, then choose the nearest benchmark.

0.12 _____   0.36 _____   0.453 _____

0.785 _____   1.007 _____

Numeration

It's Absolutely in the Cards

30 minutes to introduce the game; 10–15 minutes thereafter

OBJECTIVES

- Recognize and use negative numbers
- Write expresssions and justify using properties
- Compute using the additive inverse
- Understand absolute value

MATERIALS

- one standard deck of playing cards for each group of 2 to 3 students, or use 3" × 5" index cards to create a deck consisting of 4 sets of cards numbered from 1 to 13, two sets in black and two sets in red.
- calculators (optional)

TEACHER NOTES

- Have students investigate negative numbers using a number line. Make sure they understand that $8 + {}^-8 = 0$.

- Have students break into groups and play the card game. Be sure students record each equation they create. Students can check other students' equations when it is not their turn.

- If using a standard deck of cards, Ace = 1, Jack = 11, Queen = 12, King = 13.

EXTENSIONS

- Have students use parentheses for order of operations, meaning they may now multiply the values of the cards.

- Have students write equations using the Associative and Distributive Properties, naming the property used next to the equation they write.

- Have students use a target number other than zero when creating their equations. For example, the new number can be positive or negative.

- Let jokers, or 3" × 5" index cards marked "Wild," indicate special procedures. For example, these cards could stand for a designated power, allowing a sum to be raised to a power, such as $(2 + 3)^2 + {}^-13 + {}^-12 = 0$.

- Change the way the scoring is calculated. The player who goes out gets zero points and the other players get the value of the cards remaining in their hands, totaling the positive and negative amounts.

- For a different game, have students deal out all the cards. Students must make equations with progressively larger target numbers. The first player makes an equation totaling 0, the second player makes an equation totaling 1, the third player tries for 2, and so on. If a player cannot make the target number, that target goes to the next player. Play continues either until someone goes out by discarding the last card in his or her hand, or until all players pass on the same target number. If all players have passed on the same target number, the absolute values of the cards remaining in their hands are added together. The player with the lowest total is the winner.

▶ It's Absolutely in the Cards

**Positive and Negative
    Numbers:** 046

Integers: 047

Absolute Value: 050

**Adding with Negative
    Numbers:** 108

Inverse Elements: 224

Game Rules

a. Make a group of 2 or 3 players. Choose one player to be the dealer.

b. The dealer shuffles the cards well and deals 10 cards to each player. The remaining cards are placed in a facedown stack in the middle. Turn the top card over and place it to the side to begin the discard pile.

c. Red cards are negative and black cards are positive. The face cards and aces have the following values: Ace = 1, Jack = 11, Queen = 12, King = 13. Each player uses the cards in her or his hand to create as many addition equations that equal zero as possible. For example:

$$^-4 + {}^-6 + 8 + 2 = 0$$

The cards used to create each zero equation must be displayed face up in front of the player. Record each equation on the lines provided using correct mathematical notation.

d. When all players have played what they can, the player to the left of the dealer begins. That player picks up either the discard or the top card from the facedown stack and repeats the procedure outlined in step 3, displaying and recording each equation. A player <u>must</u> discard at the end of each turn. The discard is placed on the pile so that all cards in the discard pile can be seen. Play then passes to the next player on the left.

e. Play continues in the same way. Players can pick up more than the top card from the discard pile, but must pick up all cards on top of the desired card. The desired card must be used in an equation on that turn.

f. The round ends when one of the players goes out. To go out, a player must be able to use the last card in his or her hand as the discard.

g. The player who goes out wins the round and gets points from the other players. The sum of the absolute values of the cards remaining in the hands of the other players is awarded to the player who goes out.

h. Players can define a game to be a certain number of rounds, the winner being the player with the most points. A game may also be defined by setting a target score, such as 100. The winner is the first player to reach that goal.

Numeration

A Number by Any Other Name . . .

30–45 minutes

OBJECTIVE
• Obtain a better understanding of other numeration systems

MATERIALS
• Math Notebook Page, page 119

TEACHER NOTES
• The purpose of this activity is to explore other numeration systems, and to compare and contrast them with the system we use today. Information about these numeration systems makes a good addition to the study of the cultures in which they were developed.

EXTENSIONS
• To increase awareness of the strengths and limitations of the various number systems, have students perform each of the four basic computational operations in each system. You can choose to focus on one operation and apply it to all the number systems, or choose one number system and try each operation in that system.

• Binary Numerals are used in writing programs for computers. This has led to some new words in our vocabulary such as googol, googolplex, bits, bytes, and gigabytes. Choose some of these terms to define with the students, and discuss whether they think this is a new or developing number system.

ANSWERS
1. ∧ ∧ ∧ | | |
          | | |
          | | |

2. ⌒ ∧ ∧ ∧ | | | |
            | | | |

3. ⌒ ⌒ ⌒ | | | |
     ⌒ ⌒ | | |

4. ⌐ ♌ ♌ ⌒⌒⌒ ∧∧∧ | | |
                     ∧∧ | | |

5. 144

6. 99

7. 1110

8. < ∨ ∨ ∨
       ∨ ∨ ∨

9. ▼ ▼ ▼ ▼ ▼ ▼ < ∨ ∨ ∨ ∨
                      ∨ ∨ ∨ ∨

10. ▼ ▼ ∨ ∨ ∨
          ∨ ∨ ∨

11. 23

12. 150

13. 99

14. 182

15. XVIII

16. CXCV

17. DCXII

18. MMMXIV

19. 99

20. 5555

21. 486

22. 24

23. When a symbol for a smaller number is to the left of another symbol, it represents a difference or subtraction. MC represents 1100 and CM represents 900.

Name _____

▶ A Number by Any Other Name . . .

Whole Numbers: Place
    Value: **004**

Lining Up by Place
    Value: **008**

Number Systems: **551–558**

**References to
MATH ON CALL**

Use *Math on Call* to help you convert numbers from one numeral system to another. Use your Math Notebook Page and the back of this page if you need more space.

Egyptian Numerals—Write these numbers in the Egyptian system.

1. 39   **2.** 148

3. 507   **4.** 12,356

Write these Egyptian numbers in our system.

5. 𓎡∩∩∩∩ | | | | **6.** ∩∩∩ | | |
                                  ∩∩∩ | | |
                                  ∩∩∩ | | |

7. 𓋹𓎡∩

Babylonian Numerals—Write these numbers in the Babylonian system.

8. 16   **9.** 378

10. 126

Write these Babylonian numbers in our system.

11. ⟨⟨ ⋁⋁⋁   **12.** ⋁ ⋁ ⟨⟨⟨

13. ⋁ ⟨⟨⟨ ⋁⋁⋁⋁⋁ ⋁⋁⋁⋁   **14.** ⋁ ⋁ ⋁ ⋁⋁

Roman Numerals—Write these numbers in the Roman system.

15. 18   **16.** 195

17. 612   **18.** 3014

Write these Roman numbers in our system.

19. XCIX   **20.** V̄DLV

21. XXIV   **22.** CDLXXXVI

23. Explain the difference between MC and CM in the Roman system.

_____

_____

That's right—the Roman army is coming. I want to order 𓋹𓎡∩∩ | | | pizzas to go.

Numeration

That's Yours—This Is Mayan!

45–60 minutes

OBJECTIVES
- Obtain a better understanding of Mayan numerals
- Practice addition using the Mayan Number System

MATERIALS
- Math Notebook Page, page 119

TEACHER NOTES
- This activity introduces new information about Mayan numerals and demonstrates the process of addition in that system.

- Allowing students to use manipulatives to construct the Mayan numerals may help students understand the addition process more easily.

- For more information about the Mayan Number System, see "A Mathematics Lesson from the Mayan Civilization" in *Teaching Children Mathematics*, Vol. 5, No. 5, November 1998.

EXTENSIONS
- Demonstrate the number 1999 in our system by showing students that one way to look at the number is to define the place value of each digit and multiply by that value. So 1999 is $(1 \times 1000) + (9 \times 100) + (9 \times 10) + (9 \times 1) = 1999$. This is the same procedure used in the Mayan system. The difference is that the Mayan system uses a place value based on 20. Just as our hundreds place is 10×10, or 10^2, the Mayan four-hundreds place is 20×20, or 20^2. Our thousands place (10^3) corresponds to the eight-thousands place (20^3) in the Mayan system.

- It is likely that the symbols used in the representation of the Mayan numerals were derived from that civilization's close observance of nature. The dot may represent a rock, bean, or seed. The bar is probably a picture of an open human hand. The symbol for zero may represent a closed hand, or possibly a shell.

- Have students pretend they are the ruling body of a distant planet. They must design a number system for all the inhabitants to use. Have students decide whether they will use an additive system (like the Egyptian system) or a place-value system (like the Mayan system). They can experiment

with what number to use as the base of their system. They may also base the written symbols on things in their environment. Once the system has been designed, try out some basic calculations. Lead a discussion about the advantages and disadvantages of their system compared to the one we normally use.

ANSWERS

1.

2.

3. 18,625

4. 40,243

5.  = =

6. =

7. =

8. = =

That's Yours—This Is Mayan!

Mayan Numerals: **555**

**References to
MATH ON CALL**

eight-thousands place	(20^3)
four-hundreds place	(20^2)
twentys place	(20^1)
ones place	(20^0)

The Mayan numerals for numbers 0 to 19 are shown in *Math on Call*. To write numbers larger than 19, the Mayans stacked the numerals. Each new stack represented a place value based on 20. To make it easier to see the stacking, we'll use rectangular boxes. The table to the left shows the place value system.

This is how the number 1999 is written in the Mayan system. The numerals are built from the bottom up, so the lowest "box" is always the ones place.

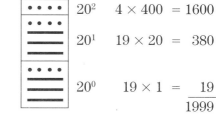

$20^2 \quad 4 \times 400 = 1600$
$20^1 \quad 19 \times 20 = 380$
$20^0 \quad 19 \times 1 = \underline{\quad 19}$
$\qquad\qquad\qquad\qquad 1999$

1. Write the Mayan numeral for 110.

2. Write the Mayan numeral for 208.

3. What number is this in our system?

_____

4. What number is this in our system?

_____

Here is how to add 21 and 44 in the Mayan system.

 (1×20)
(1×1)

a. Write each number in Mayan notation. The number 21 is one times 20 plus one 1.

(2×20)
(4×1)

b. The number 44 is two times 20 plus four ones.

c. To add, position the two numbers next to each other, one number in each column.

(3×20)
(5×1)

d. Complete the addition by adding the dots and bars within the rows. Show the result in one column.

Remember!
- 5 dots equal one bar.
- 4 bars equal one dot in the next higher box.

 (1×400)
(0×20)
(19×1)

- Each place value must contain a symbol. Remember to use the symbol for zero if necessary. For example, here is how the number 419 is written in the Mayan system.

On your Math Notebook Page, do these addition problems using the Mayan system.

5. $30 + 70$ **6.** $56 + 25$ **7.** $549 + 813$ **8.** $203 + 302$

Can You Imagic That?

30 minutes

OBJECTIVES

- Compute with whole numbers
- Translate computation into algebraic expressions
- Justify reasoning with algebraic notation

MATERIALS

- Math Notebook Page, page 119
- colored cubes and algebra tiles (optional)

TEACHER NOTES

- This activity featuring simple computation can be used as a quick review of basic procedures. It is also a good activity to use when writing and evaluating expressions.

- The pictures provided in Case #1 develop the concept of variables without using letters and math symbols. Algebra tiles or colored cubes can be used to define the operations. The manipulatives provide a link to the more abstract algebraic expressions.

- When using algebraic notation, be sure students know how to apply the Distributive Properties and use the correct order of operations.

EXTENSIONS

- Many number and card tricks have their basis in number theory. Students can analyze these tricks to discover the underlying math that explains the trick.

- Have students look for books of number puzzles to find other "tricks" to share with the class.

ANSWERS

1. Yes.

2. Write a number that is easy to remember. (x)

3. Double it. ($2x$)

4. Add 15 to the product. ($2x + 15$)

5. Triple the new answer. ($3(2x + 15)$ which is $6x + 45$)

6. Add 33. ($6x + 78$)

7. Divide by 6. ($x + 13$)

8. Subtract the original number. ($x + 13 - x = 13$)

9. Check student explanations for accuracy.

10. You may want to try out some of the student puzzles with the class.

▶ Can You Imagic That?

Dr. Wise Won claims to be a math psychic. She gives the students in her class two sample "tricks" to prove her claim. Your job is to find the math behind the magic.

Case #1

| Select a number that is easy to remember. □ |
| Multiply the number by 3. □□□ |
| Add 15 to the product. □□□ ⊞⊞⊞ |
| Multiply the total by 2. □□□ ⊞⊞⊞ □□□ ⊞⊞⊞ |
| Divide the product by 6. □⊞ □⊞ □⊞ (□⊞) □⊞ □⊞ |
| Subtract the original number. ⊞ |

1. Try starting with different numbers. Do you get the same

answer every time? _____

For Case #2, Dr. Wise Won has given you her special symbols. Your job is to create the directions for each step. On your Math Notebook Page, number each step and write the directions. Then try writing each step using math symbols and variables. This can help you discover why the "trick" works no matter what number you start with.

Case #2 "Wise Won Is Unlucky?"

2. △

3. △△

4. △△ ⊞⊞⊞

5. △△ ⊞⊞⊞
   △△ ⊞⊞⊞
   △△ ⊞⊞⊞

6. △△ ⊞⊞⊞   ⊞⊞III
   △△ ⊞⊞⊞   ⊞⊞
   △△ ⊞⊞⊞   ⊞⊞

7. △ ⊞⊞III   △ ⊞⊞III
   △ ⊞⊞III   △ ⊞⊞III
   (△ ⊞⊞III)   △ ⊞⊞III

8. ⊞⊞III

Your answer will be 13.

9. On your Math Notebook Page, write a brief explanation of how each case works.

10. Create your own number puzzle.

Primarily Patterns

45–60 minutes

OBJECTIVES

• Determine which numbers are prime
• Find patterns for composite numbers

MATERIALS

• crayons or colored pencils
• Math Notebook Page, page 119

TEACHER NOTES

• In *Math on Call* there is a 10 table in item number 058. Point out to the students that the ones digit in each column in this 10 table is always the same because our decimal system is based on 10. In the 6 table on the student page, the pattern of the ones digits is not the same.

• As the students follow the procedure, point out that after they have crossed out all the multiples of 2 (the first prime number), half of the table is crossed out.

• After crossing out all the multiples of 3, point out that all the numbers in the sixth column are marked with two colors. Explain that this is because all the numbers in that column are multiples of both 2 and 3. Notice that two-thirds of the table is now crossed out.

EXTENSIONS

• Create tables based on rows of 4, 5, 7, 8, 9, and 11. The basic procedure remains the same, but the resulting patterns are different in each case. You can organize the students into groups for this activity and assign a different table for each group. The groups report the patterns they discover to the class and the class can compare the patterns among all the tables.

• Ask students to identify all the twin primes in the 6 table. (See *Math on Call* Glossary, 594.)

• A reverse prime is a prime number that is also prime when its digits are reversed. For example, 17 and 71 are reverse primes. How many other reverse primes can be found on the 6 table?

ANSWERS

1. The number 1 is neither prime nor composite since it has only one factor.

2. The first prime number is 2. The multiples of 2 appear in the second, fourth, and sixth columns.

3. Composite numbers. Any number that is a multiple of another number is a composite number.

4. The multiples of 3 appear in the third and sixth columns. The multiples of 5 appear diagonally down to the left while the multiples of 7 appear diagonally down to the right. The multiples of 11 and 13 also create diagonals moving down in opposite directions.

5. The prime numbers appear most often in the first and fifth columns.

6. 953 is a prime number and will appear in the fifth column. Since most of the prime numbers in the fifth column have a 3 in the ones place, it is a good prediction that 953 will be a prime number.

7. The table can be continued indefinitely. Since most prime numbers appear in either the first or fifth columns, just determining which column a number will appear in will give a good indication of whether it is prime or not.

▶ **Primarily Patterns**

Prime numbers can be sifted out of a table. Eratosthenes was a Greek mathematician who is credited with first identifying the prime numbers by using a table. The table he used is called the Sieve of Eratosthenes. *Math on Call* shows a table based on rows of 10 in item number 058.

Prime Numbers: **058**
One Is Not Prime: **059**
Composite Numbers: **060**
Multiples: **067**
Divisibility: **069**
Twin Primes: **594**

References to MATH ON CALL

PROCEDURE

Use the sieve based on rows of 6 shown on this page. Sift the table for prime numbers by following these steps:

a. Place a star on 1.

b. Circle the first prime number. Use one color to cross out all the numbers that are multiples of that number.

c. Circle the next prime number and cross out all its multiples in a second color.

d. Continue circling prime numbers and crossing out the multiples of each in a different color. Stop when you have crossed out all the multiples of 13.

e. All circled numbers and all numbers that have not been crossed out are prime numbers.

Answer these questions on your Math Notebook Page.

1. You marked the number 1 with a star. What is special about the number 1?

2. What is the first (lowest) prime number? In what columns do its multiples appear?

3. Are these multiples prime or composite numbers? How do you know?

4. Describe the patterns created by the multiples of 3, 5, 7, 11, and 13.

5. In which columns do the prime numbers appear?

6. Can you predict in which column the number 953 will appear? Will it be a prime or composite number?

7. How can this table help you predict whether any number is prime or composite?

1	2	3	4	5	6
7	8	9	10	11	12
13	14	15	16	17	18
19	20	21	22	23	24
25	26	27	28	29	30
31	32	33	34	35	36
37	38	39	40	41	42
43	44	45	46	47	48
49	50	51	52	53	54
55	56	57	58	59	60
61	62	63	64	65	66
67	68	69	70	71	72
73	74	75	76	77	78
79	80	81	82	83	84
85	86	87	88	89	90
91	92	93	94	95	96
97	98	99	100	101	102
103	104	105	106	107	108
109	110	111	112	113	114
115	116	117	118	119	120
121	122	123	124	125	126
127	128	129	130	131	132
133	134	135	136	137	138
139	140	141	142	143	144
145	146	147	148	149	150

Very Interesting, My Dear

45–60 minutes

OBJECTIVES

- Use a calculator with exponents
- Record, organize and analyze data
- Look for patterns
- Increase awareness of how fast numbers grow when increased exponentially

MATERIALS

- calculators
- Math Notebook Page, page 119

TEACHER NOTES

- Students should be able to use a calculator to raise a number to an indicated power. Point out that how this is done can vary from one calculator to another. Also, inform students that some calculator displays will not show all the digits of very large numbers. They should also know whether they have an exact answer or a scientific notation answer.

EXTENSION

- Have students take another look at the "Boring Exponent Families" to see if a more interesting pattern can be found by looking at different place values. For example, in the table showing powers of 5, notice that the tens value is always 2. The pattern in the hundreds place is 1, 6. If the chart is extended, there are more patterns to be found. So 5 is not such a "Boring" number after all. Try this same activity with the number 11.

ANSWERS

1.

Powers of 2	
2^1	2
2^2	4
2^3	8
2^4	16
2^5	32
2^6	64
2^7	128
2^8	256
2^9	512
2^{10}	1024

2.

Powers of 3	
3^1	3
3^2	9
3^3	27
3^4	81
3^5	243
3^6	729
3^7	2187
3^8	6561
3^9	19,683
3^{10}	59,049

3.

Powers of 4	
4^1	4
4^2	16
4^3	64
4^4	256
4^5	1024
4^6	4096
4^7	16,384
4^8	65,536
4^9	262,144
4^{10}	1,048,576

Powers of 5	
5^1	5
5^2	25
5^3	125
5^4	625
5^5	3125
5^6	15,625
5^7	78,125
5^8	390,625
5^9	1,953,125
5^{10}	9,765,625

Powers of 6	
6^1	6
6^2	36
6^3	216
6^4	1296
6^5	7776
6^6	46,656
6^7	279,936
6^8	1,679,616
6^9	10,077,696
6^{10}	60,466,176

Powers of 7	
7^1	7
7^2	49
7^3	343
7^4	2401
7^5	16,807
7^6	117,649
7^7	823,543
7^8	5,764,801
7^9	40,353,607
7^{10}	282,475,249

Powers of 8	
8^1	8
8^2	64
8^3	512
8^4	4096
8^5	32,768
8^6	262,144
8^7	2,097,152
8^8	16,777,216
8^9	134,217,728
8^{10}	1,073,741,824

Powers of 9	
9^1	9
9^2	81
9^3	729
9^4	6561
9^5	59,049
9^6	531,441
9^7	4,782,969
9^8	43,046,721
9^9	387,420,489
9^{10}	3,486,784,401

Powers of 10	
10^1	10
10^2	100
10^3	1000
10^4	10,000
10^5	100,000
10^6	1,000,000
10^7	10,000,000
10^8	100,000,000
10^9	1,000,000,000
10^{10}	10,000,000,000

4. Powers of 5, 6, and 10   **5.** Powers of 4 and 9   **6.** Powers of 2, 3, 7, and 8

7. 5   **8.** 9   **9.** 9   **10.** 2   **11.** 6   **12.** 5

▶ **Very Interesting, My Dear**

Complete these tables showing Powers of 2 and Powers of 3.

Ways of Writing Whole Numbers: **005**

Positive Exponents: **071**

Using a Calculator with Exponents: **075**

Using a Table of Powers and Roots: **079**

Perfect Powers: **083**

Sample Size: **266**

Make a Table or an Organized List: **480**

References to MATH ON CALL

1.

Powers of 2	
2^1	2
2^2	4
2^3	8
2^4	
2^5	
2^6	
2^7	
2^8	
2^9	
2^{10}	

2.

Powers of 3	
3^1	
3^2	
3^3	
3^4	
3^5	
3^6	
3^7	
3^8	
3^9	
3^{10}	

3. Use both sides of your Math Notebook Page to make similar tables to show the powers of 4, 5, 6, 7, 8, 9, and 10.

Look for patterns in the ones digits in each table. We can use nicknames for these patterns.

"Boring Exponent Families" have a single digit that repeats in the ones place.

"Interesting Exponent Families" have a repetition pattern of 2 digits in the ones place, for example 3, 5, 3, 5.

"Exciting Exponent Families" have a repetition pattern of 4 digits in the ones place, for example 2, 3, 4, 5, 2, 3, 4, 5.

4. Which tables show Boring Exponent Families?

_____

5. Which tables show Interesting Exponent Families?

_____

6. Which tables show Exciting Exponent Families?

_____

Using only your tables, predict what digit will appear in the ones place in each of the following.

7. 5^{31} _____   **8.** 7^{42} _____   **9.** 9^{27} _____

10. 2^{212} _____   **11.** 98^4 _____   **12.** 205^{17} _____

Tessellating Factors

45–60
minutes

OBJECTIVES

- Compare regular and semi-regular tessellations
- Create tessellations using number theory and factors of 360

MATERIALS

- calculators
- pattern blocks
- 1 cm Grid Paper, page 121

TEACHER NOTES

- Tiling of the plane is an opportunity to relate geometry and number theory. In this activity, students will examine the factors of 360 and the measures of interior angles of regular polygons to create regular and semi-regular tessellations.

- Pattern blocks are an excellent manipulative for students to use during this activity. Students should first tile the tops of their desks with pattern blocks to practice completely covering a surface. Then they can move on to covering a surface with only regular polygons.

- You may want students to measure the interior angles of each of the pattern blocks, and determine which of the pattern blocks are regular and which are not.

EXTENSIONS

- Investigate the art of M. C. Escher. Some of his repetitive patterns are based on tessellations of squares or hexagons.

- Investigate the computational proof that there are only 8 semi-regular tessellations.

2. 1, 2, 3, 4, 5, 6, 8, 9, 10, 12, 15, 18, 20, 24, 30, 36, 40, 45, ⟨60,⟩ 72, ⟨90,⟩ ⟨120,⟩ 180, 360

3. Four squares: $4 \times 90° = 360°$; three hexagons: $3 \times 120° = 360°$; six equilateral triangles: $6 \times 60° = 360°$.

4. a. One equilateral triangle and two regular 12-sided polygons (dodecagons): $60° + 2(150°) = 360°$.

b. One equilateral triangle, one square, one hexagon, and another square: $60° + 90° + 120° + 90° = 360°$.

c. One hexagon and four equilateral triangles: $120° + 4(60°) = 360°$.

d. One regular 12-sided polygon (dodecagon), one hexagon, and one square: $150° + 120° + 90° = 360°$.

e. Three equilateral triangles and 2 squares: $3(60°) + 2(90°) = 360°$.

ANSWERS

1.

Number of sides of a regular polygon	3	4	5	6	7	8	9	10	11	12
Measure of one interior angle, rounded to the nearest hundredth	60°	90°	108°	120°	128.57°	135°	140°	144°	147.27°	150°

▶ **Tessellating Factors**

Factors: **056**

Central Angles: **340**

Interior Angles: **341**

Sums of Interior Angles of Polygons: **342**

Tessellations: **391**

Guess, Check, and Revise: **478**

Make a Table or an Organized List: **480**

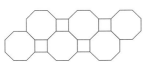

References to MATH ON CALL

Artists and interior designers tile planes to create attractive patterns. Mathematicians tile planes using factors and number theory.

1. Regular polygons are equiangular. Use the information in *Math on Call*, item number 342, to complete this chart.

Number of sides of a regular polygon	3	4	5	6	7	8	9	10	11	12
Measure of one interior angle, rounded to the nearest hundredth										

2. List the factors of 360. Circle the factors that could represent the measure in degrees of one interior angle of a regular polygon.

_____

_____

3. A tessellation is the tiling of a plane surface so that it is completely covered. A regular tessellation is created by the repetition of the same regular polygon. In order for a regular polygon to tessellate, the measure of its interior angle must be a factor of 360. Use the factors of 360 to determine which polygons will form a regular tessellation. Write the regular tessellations, then sketch them on your grid paper.

_____

_____

4. A semi-regular tessellation involves more than one regular polygon. To find arrangements of polygons that will create semi-regular tessellations, use guess and check. Try adding the measures of interior angles of regular polygons or multiples of the measures of interior angles in order to get a sum of 360°. For example, $90° + 2(135°) = 360°$. So a square and 2 regular octagons will tessellate. Also, $(2 \times 60°) + (2 \times 120°) = 360°$. So 2 equilateral triangles and 2 regular hexagons will tessellate.

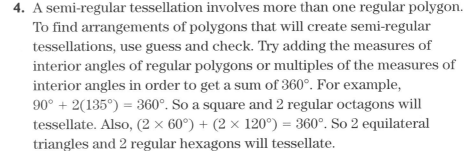

Find 5 other combinations of regular polygons that could make a semi-regular tessellation. Use guess and check to find them, and then arrange them using pattern blocks. You may want to use the pattern blocks to build them first, and then show why they work mathematically.

That Light Was Red

30-45 minutes

OBJECTIVE

• Apply problem-solving strategies

MATERIALS

• calculators
• stop watch (optional)

TEACHER NOTES

• Allow students to make pictures or use models to determine solutions to this problem.

• You may want students to work in groups for this activity. Acting out the given scenario may help students visualize the traffic patterns.

EXTENSIONS

• Have students time traffic lights in their neighborhoods. Exactly how long are they green? Yellow? Red? Do the times vary depending on the intersection? If so, what is different about the intersections?

• Have students time cars at a four-way stop. If there are five cars at each corner and you are in the fifth car, how long would it take you to get through the intersection?

• Students can compare the cycles of one traffic light at different times of day. Is it programmed to change based on the amount of traffic?

ANSWERS

1. To calculate this, add the duration of the green and yellow lights in all locations other than the location where the car is waiting. Add 6 seconds for delays.

2. One full cycle of a light is 90 seconds.

3. The delay occurs only for cars going straight because that traffic is typically going much faster and will need more time to stop.

4. If no cars are in the eastbound left-turn lane, drivers in the westbound straight-ahead lane would get the longer green light. It would be both the duration of the eastbound left-turn lane green and yellow lights and the duration of the westbound straight-ahead lane green light. (12 seconds + 4 seconds + 22 seconds = 38 seconds)

5. Since you are traveling at 30 mph, you are traveling 1 mile every 2 minutes. Therefore, the duration of a cycle is 2 minutes, or 120 seconds.

Direction of Traffic	Location of Light	Duration of Green	Duration of Yellow	Duration of Red
North/South	Left-turn	12 seconds	4 seconds	74 seconds
North/South	Straight-ahead	22 seconds	4 seconds	64 seconds
East/West	Left-turn	12 seconds	4 seconds	74 seconds
East/West	Straight-ahead	22 seconds	4 seconds	64 seconds

▶ That Light Was Red

Make a Model or a
  Diagram: 483

Look for Patterns: 484

Make a Plan: 488

The Customary
  System: 536

**References to
MATH ON CALL**

Did you know that the timing of all traffic lights is not the same? Some lights have set times for each side of an intersection. Some lights start by checking the left-turn lane. If there are no cars in the left-turn lane, then the opposite side going straight gets a longer green light.

The table shows the duration of green and yellow lights for four different traffic lights at one intersection with straight-ahead and left-turn lanes. The lights are designed so that only one lane of cars has the right-of-way at a time. There is a 3-second delay between the beginning of the red light in the straight-ahead lane and the beginning of the green light in the next left-turn lane.

1. Calculate the duration of the red light for each of the traffic lights.

Direction of Traffic	Location of Light	Duration of Green	Duration of Yellow	Duration of Red
North/South	Left-turn	12 seconds	4 seconds	
North/South	Straight-ahead	22 seconds	4 seconds	
East/West	Left-turn	12 seconds	4 seconds	
East/West	Straight-ahead	22 seconds	4 seconds	

2. How long does it take from the time a light turns green to the next time the same light turns green?

_____

3. Why do you think the delay occurs only after the beginning of a red light for cars going straight?

_____

4. If there are no cars in the eastbound left-turn lane, how does this affect the duration of the green light for the westbound straight-ahead lane? How long would the green light be?

_____

_____

5. There are six lights within one mile on a straight road traveling north in town. Traffic travels at 30 mph. You want to follow the road and not stop for any of the lights. Each light is timed so that if you arrive at one light when it just turns green, all the lights will turn green as you arrive at them. For this set of lights, what is the duration of a complete cycle for each light?

_____

_____

Decimals on a Roll

OBJECTIVES

- Estimate sums
- Add with decimals
- Relate fractions to decimals

MATERIALS

- Grocery store ads (optional)

30–45 minutes

TEACHER NOTES

- Make sure students realize that they will need to calculate the number of adults attending the picnic.

- Discuss the fact that decimal units for pounds can be confusing. One-half pound equals 8 ounces, but 0.8 pound is not one-half pound.

- This activity readily lends itself to be graded using a rubric.
  Copper: Unable to understand the problem or to provide a solution.
  Bronze: Able to pick a quantity of food that would serve everyone.
  Silver: Selects the items which allow the least amount of waste.
  Gold: Defends answers fully both with mathematical models and written responses.
  As students move up the rubric, they should be able to demonstrate the previous level(s) in their process.

EXTENSIONS

- Use grocery store ads to find the price of ground beef and hamburger rolls. Have students calculate the cost of making 37 hamburgers for 18 children and 19 adults.

- Change the problem from hamburgers to hot dogs. Hot dogs are 6, 8, or 12 inches long and come in packages of 6, 8, or 10. Hot dog rolls come in packages of 6 or 8.

- Complete the menu for the picnic. Have students talk to the school cafeteria staff about serving sizes. Then have them determine how much salad, beverage, and dessert they would need to feed 18 children and 19 adults.

ANSWERS

1.

Approximate Number of Adult Servings	5	4	3	2	1	0
Approximate Number of Child Servings	0	2	3	4	5	7

2. 8.35 lbs

3. $1.20 + 1.78 + 2.91 + 2.46 = 8.35$, or $2.27 + 3.15 + 2.91 = 8.33$

4. Two 4-roll packages and five 6-roll packages. $(2 \times 4) + (5 \times 6) = 38$, with only one extra roll.

▶ Decimals on a Roll

It's time once again for the annual family reunion picnic. Thirty-seven people are coming to the picnic. Of the 37 people, 18 are children.

This year you are in charge of the hamburgers. Your mom says adult-size hamburgers are $\frac{1}{4}$ pound and child-size hamburgers are $\frac{1}{5}$ pound.

Using Compatible Numbers to Estimate Sums: **093**

Front-End Estimation of Sums: **094**

Adjusting Front-End Estimation of Sums: **095**

Proportion: **428**

References to MATH ON CALL

1. In the table below, write all the different ways you can divide one 1.41-pound package of lean ground beef to make hamburgers for adults and children.

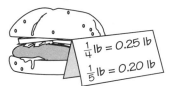

$\frac{1}{4}$ lb = 0.25 lb
$\frac{1}{5}$ lb = 0.20 lb

Approximate Number of Adult Servings					
Approximate Number of Child Servings					

With all the other food planned for the picnic, you estimate that one hamburger per person will be enough. The morning of the picnic you go to the grocery store to buy the ground beef and hamburger rolls.

2. How much ground beef should you buy so each adult and child can have one hamburger? _____

At the meat counter you find packages of ground beef with the following weights:

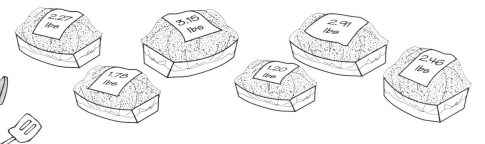

2.27 lbs   3.15 lbs   2.91 lbs   2.46 lbs   1.78 lbs   1.20 lbs

3. Look at the selection of available packages of ground beef.

   Decide which packages to buy. _____

   _____

4. In the bread aisle you discover that hamburger rolls are sold four to a package and six to a package. Decide how many packages of each to buy. Defend your answer.

   _____ 4-roll packages   _____ 6-roll packages

Looney Larry Loses Logic

30–45 minutes

OBJECTIVES

- Convert fractions to benchmark fractions
- Use benchmark fractions to compute
- Analyze statistical data
- Estimate ratios and proportions

MATERIALS

- Math Notebook Page, page 119

TEACHER NOTES

- Benchmark fractions are used as reference points to estimate computation with fractions. In this activity the benchmarks are also used to find reasonable substitutes for complicated fractions. "Unfriendly" fractions encourage students to estimate. "Unfriendly" fractions can become "friendly" fractions by using benchmark fractions to estimate.

- Review computing with fractions. For example:

$\frac{1}{4}$ of 40 = 40 ÷ 4

$\frac{1}{5}$ of 65 = 65 ÷ 5

$\frac{1}{3}$ of 36 = 36 ÷ 3

- Make sure that students can take this a step further.

If $\frac{1}{4}$ of 40 = 10, then $\frac{3}{4}$ of 40 is 3 × 10, or 30.

If $\frac{1}{5}$ of 65 = 13, then $\frac{2}{5}$ of 65 is 2 × 13, or 26.

If $\frac{1}{3}$ of 36 = 12, then $\frac{2}{3}$ of 36 is 2 × 12, or 24.

- Make sure that students understand that

$\frac{21}{33} \approx \frac{2}{3}$

$\frac{39}{51} \approx \frac{4}{5}$

$\frac{8}{33} \approx \frac{1}{4}$

- This is a good time to discuss a quick-check method for addition. To check the total number of people actually polled by Looney Larry, use the ones digits only (2, 7, 7, 1, 8) from his tally sheet. Eliminate any digits whose sum is 10, such as 8 + 2 or 7 + 2 + 1. Then add the remaining digits. In this case the remaining digits total 15. This means that the digit in the ones place should be a 5.

EXTENSIONS

- Give students this second scenario: A survey of 21 students was conducted to determine which foods from the cafeteria were favorites. Eleven students liked pizza best; 3 favored hamburgers; 5 preferred tacos, and 2 liked egg rolls. Project the numbers for your school.

- Provide students with some fractions and have them create the scenario. If students can write and solve their own problem, the level of understanding is higher than just "doing the math." Use a rubric for scoring. The rubric allows for creativity as well as understanding of mathematical concepts.

ANSWERS

1. $\frac{32}{43}$ is about $\frac{3}{4}$, so $\frac{32}{43}$ of 100 ≈ 75.
2. $\frac{67}{99}$ is about $\frac{2}{3}$, so $\frac{67}{99}$ of 120 ≈ 80.
3. $\frac{9}{39}$ is about $\frac{1}{4}$, so $\frac{9}{39}$ of 196 ≈ 50.
4. $\frac{11}{21}$ is about $\frac{1}{2}$, so $\frac{11}{21}$ of 78 ≈ 40.
5. $\frac{3}{11}$ is about $\frac{3}{10}$, so $\frac{3}{11}$ of 290 ≈ 90.
6. A variety of answers are acceptable for this problem. One set of answers might be:

$\frac{22}{85} \approx \frac{1}{4}$ of 450 ≈ 110

$\frac{37}{85} \approx \frac{1}{2}$ of 450 ≈ 225

$\frac{7}{85} \approx \frac{1}{10}$ of 450 ≈ 45

$\frac{11}{85} \approx \frac{1}{8}$ of 450 ≈ 55

$\frac{8}{85} \approx \frac{1}{10}$ of 450 ≈ 45

Note that the sum of these estimates is 480. The students' numbers will probably not add up to 450 people upon the first calculation either. Discuss strategies for deciding what adjustments can be made to each category to make a total of 450.

7. Answers will vary. Be sure to check students' use of benchmark fractions for reasonableness.

▶ Looney Larry Loses Logic

**References to
MATH ON CALL**

Try these problems. Remember to use benchmarks and estimate.

For example, $\frac{21}{33}$ is about $\frac{2}{3}$, so $\frac{21}{33}$ of 60 ≈ 40.

1. $\frac{32}{43}$ is about _____ , so $\frac{32}{43}$ of 100 ≈ _____ .

2. $\frac{67}{99}$ is about _____ , so $\frac{67}{99}$ of 120 ≈ _____ .

3. $\frac{9}{39}$ is about _____ , so $\frac{9}{39}$ of 196 ≈ _____ .

4. $\frac{11}{21}$ is about _____ , so $\frac{11}{21}$ of 78 ≈ _____ .

5. $\frac{3}{11}$ is about _____ , so $\frac{3}{11}$ of 290 ≈ _____ .

6. Looney Larry was hired by his Uncle Fred to take
   an opinion poll on some new candy bars. He was
   to report to the mall at 9:00 Saturday morning
   and stay until 450 people had been polled. At
   noon he was exhausted and could only
   think of the fun he was missing. Larry
   counted 85 people polled on his
   tally sheet. He knew he was not
   done, but decided to project the
   numbers to save time. Here are
   the numbers Larry had when
   he stopped.

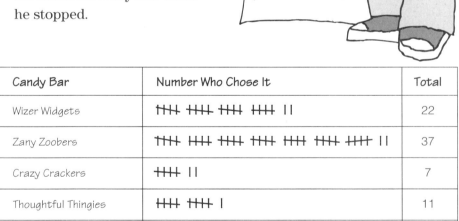

Which is
your favorite?

Candy Bar	Number Who Chose It	Total
Wizer Widgets	‖‖‖ ‖‖‖ ‖‖‖ ‖‖‖ ‖‖	22
Zany Zoobers	‖‖‖ ‖‖‖ ‖‖‖ ‖‖‖ ‖‖‖ ‖‖‖ ‖‖‖ ‖‖	37
Crazy Crackers	‖‖‖ ‖‖	7
Thoughtful Thingies	‖‖‖ ‖‖‖ ‖	11
None	‖‖‖ ‖‖‖	8

Use benchmark fractions to create Looney Larry's projected survey
to match a count of 450 people. Show your work and your results on
your Math Notebook Page.

7. Take a quick survey of favorites in your classroom. Use your data
   and benchmark fractions to project numbers for your whole
   grade level.

46

On the Fence . . .

OBJECTIVES

• Understand factors
• Use an alternative algorithm for multiplication

MATERIALS

30–45 minutes

TEACHER NOTES

These steps describe how to use the lattice.

• Place the factors on the top and right sides of the lattice. In the first problem, the factors are 4159 and 83.

• Above and below the diagonal of each cell, place the multiplication fact for the product of each row and column, for example, $9 \times 8 = 72$. The seven goes above the diagonal line and the two goes below the diagonal line.

• Add along the diagonals.

• Regroup as needed.

EXTENSIONS

• Give students a completed lattice and have them determine the factors. This will require them to look for factoring patterns.

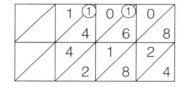

The factors in this example are 734 and 26.

• Have students create their own problems like the one above with the factors missing. They can exchange papers to solve one another's problems.

• Explore with students what happens when multiplying one or two numbers with a decimal using the lattice method.

ANSWERS

1. 4159 and 83.

2. The product of pairs of digits.

3. The tens digit is above the diagonal line and the ones digit is below it.

4. The tens column is the second diagonal from the right.

5. Addition is completed along the diagonals.

6. The circled numbers represent the regrouping when the diagonal addition is completed.

7.

		5	9	7	8	
		1 ① 5	2 ② 7	2 ① 1	2 ① 4	3
		3 5	6 3	4 9	5 6	7
2	2	1 ,	1	8	6	

These steps describe how the second method works.

• The factors are placed on the top and left sides of the grid.

• Each factor is written in expanded form (96 becomes 90 and 6).

• Multiply each number, writing the products in the appropriate boxes.

• List all the products and add.

8. $15 \times 15 = 225$

9. $38 \times 86 = 3268$

10. $93 \times 42 = 3906$

▶ **On the Fence . . .**

This lattice method for multiplication is an alternative to the methods shown in item number 154 in *Math on Call*. Analyze this lattice multiplication to answer the following questions.

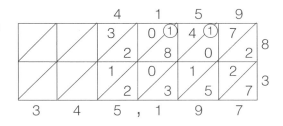

1. What are the two factors? _____

2. What do the numbers in the squares represent? _____

3. Which place value goes above the diagonal line? _____

4. Where is the tens place in this multiplication? _____

5. What operation is completed along the diagonals? _____

6. What do the numbers in the circles represent? _____

7. Here is an empty grid. Use it to find the product of 5978×37.

Here is another grid for multiplication. Compare its use to the lattice method above.

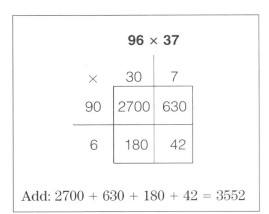

96 × 37

×	30	7
90	2700	630
6	180	42

Add: $2700 + 630 + 180 + 42 = 3552$

On the back of this page, draw three empty grids like this one and try the following problems:

8. 15×15 9. 38×86 10. 93×42

Get a Half-Life!

30–45 minutes

OBJECTIVES

- Calculate with negative exponents
- Demonstrate understanding of half-life

MATERIALS

- calculators (optional)

TEACHER NOTES

- For most students, understanding negative exponents can seem very abstract. Connecting their use with the real-world phenomenon of half-life, or exponential decay, makes the concept easier to grasp. In this activity, students practice on a problem where the numbers are manageable.

7. $\frac{1}{32}$ remains after 2 hours 15 minutes (135 minutes).

8. 0.03125 and 2^{-5}.

ANSWERS

1. 1 yard = 3 feet

2. 1.5 yards = 4.5 feet

3. 0.9 yard = 2.7 feet

4.

Shot number	0	1	2	3	4	5	6	7	8	9
Distance remaining (in yards)	240	120	60	30	15	7.5	3.75	1.875	0.9875	sinks ball

5. It will take nine shots to sink the ball.

6.

Number of half-life	Time lapsed	Fraction remaining	Decimal form	Exponential form
0	0 minutes	$\frac{1}{1}$	1.0	2^0
1	27 minutes	$\frac{1}{2}$	0.5	2^{-1}
2	54 minutes	$\frac{1}{4}$	0.25	2^{-2}
3	81 minutes	$\frac{1}{8}$	0.125	2^{-3}
4	108 minutes	$\frac{1}{16}$	0.0625	2^{-4}
5	135 minutes	$\frac{1}{32}$	0.03125	2^{-5}

▶ Get a Half-Life!

Find the equivalent measures.

1. 1 yard = _____ feet   **2.** 1.5 yards = _____ feet

3. 0.9 yard = _____ feet

Negative Exponents: **073**

Trends: **310**

Extrapolation: **311**

The Customary System: **536**

References to MATH ON CALL

Allen enjoys playing golf, but wishes he could play better. Every time he hits the ball, it only goes half the distance to the hole. The only exception is when he is within four feet of the hole. He always sinks putts that are less than four feet.

4. Hole 8 is 240 yards long. Complete the table to the left.

5. How many shots will it take Allen to sink his golf ball? _____

While this description does not match how golf is played in real life, the pattern developed in the table does exist. Scientists use this pattern to calculate what they call "half-life." In physics, half-life is the time required for one half of a radioactive material to decay. During the next half-life, half of the remaining radioactive material decays. The pattern continually repeats. As the amount of remaining radioactive material approaches zero, there is a point where scientists consider it immeasurable.

The half-life of Lead-214 is 27 minutes. This means that every 27 minutes, half of the radioactive material in Lead-214 has decayed.

6. Complete the table below to see how much Lead-214 remains after each half-life.

Shot number	Distance remaining (in yards)
0	240
1	120

Number of half-life	Time lapsed	Fraction remaining	Decimal form	Exponential form
0	0 minutes	$\frac{1}{1}$	1.0	2^0
1	27 minutes	$\frac{1}{2}$	0.5	2^{-1}
2				
3				
4				
5				

7. What fractional part of Lead-214 is left after 2 hours 15 minutes of decay? _____

8. What are the corresponding decimal and exponential forms of this amount? _____ and _____

Computation

Any Leftovers?

OBJECTIVE

• Analyze remainders

MATERIALS

30–45 minutes

TEACHER NOTES

• This activity gives an application of divisibility rules, used to plan the layout of a yearbook.

  As in other real-world applications, remind students that fractional parts of photographs will not make sense in a yearbook.

• Encourage students to use the suggestions provided in item number 069 of *Math on Call* to determine the divisibility of numbers. Students should do the division by 7 and 8 with paper and pencil. The use of calculators is not recommended with this activity.

EXTENSIONS

• Students can design a division situation where the remainders are important. Ideas might include the seating of many people at a dinner party with several tables, or the distribution of a small number of pamphlets to each classroom in your school. Both of these situations will require the students to determine how remainders must be treated when applied to the real world.

• Students should compare and contrast situations when items in the real world can be split into fractional parts with situations where fractional parts make no sense.

ANSWERS

1. See the table below.

Number of pages	Number of pictures per page
4	120
5	96
6	80
7	68 R4
8	60
9	53 R3
10	48

2. See the table below.

Number of pictures per page	Number of pictures per row with 6 rows	Number of pictures per row with 7 rows	Number of pictures per row with 8 rows	Number of pictures per row with 9 rows
120	20	17 R1	15	13 R3
96	16	13 R5	12	10 R6
80	13 R2	11 R3	10	8 R8
60	10	8 R4	7 R4	6 R6
48	8	6 R6	6	5 R3

3. There should be 10 pages with 48 pictures on each page. There could be 8 rows of 6 pictures, or 6 rows of 8 pictures.

▶ Any Leftovers?

Factors: **056**

Divisibility: **069**

Interpreting Quotients
and Remainders: **182**

**References to
MATH ON CALL**

Maria and Lyn Sing are dividing student photographs among the pages of the yearbook. They have 480 student photographs in one grade to arrange on the pages. The book map allows 4–10 pages for this one grade. The graphic designer suggests that the pages should be balanced, yet allow room for candid shots. He also suggests that there should be from 4 to 8 pictures in a row, and between 6 and 9 rows on a page. Maria and Lyn Sing have asked you to help them with the layout.

1. The 480 student photographs should be divided evenly among the pages. Your first job is to decide how many pages can be used. Use divisibility rules to determine the number of pages that are possibilities. Fill in the table to organize your plan for the layout.

Number of pages	Number of pictures per page
4	
5	
6	
7	
8	
9	
10	

2. Now list the possibilities in this table. For each possibility, find the number of pictures per row for arrangements using between 6 and 9 rows on each page.

Number of pictures per page	Number of pictures per row with 6 rows	Number of pictures per row with 7 rows	Number of pictures per row with 8 rows	Number of pictures per row with 9 rows

3. What are the possible layouts that will have an equal number of pictures in each row and between 4 and 8 pictures in each row? _____

_____

_____

Computation

Euro Dollar, I'm a Currency

30–45 minutes

OBJECTIVE

• Compute and compare currencies of various European countries

MATERIALS

• calculators (optional)

TEACHER NOTES

• Countries in the European Union have gotten together to create a single monetary system to stabilize exchange rates between currencies. This will facilitate trade between countries as well as make currency exchanges much simpler for travelers and business people. The currency is called the European Currency Unit (ECU), and is commonly known as the Euro.

• Students will need to use the exchange rates provided to determine equivalent amounts of money between currencies. These exchange rates extend several place values for some currencies, but reflect what is printed in the newspaper.

• The exchange rates provided are from September 11, 1998. Currency exchange rates change daily.

ANSWERS

1. The answers are rounded to the nearest hundredth, as most monetary units do not extend past that point.

Country Visited	**$1.00** U.S. equals:	**$15.00** U.S. equals:
Belgium	34.900 Francs	523.50 Francs
France	5.6790 Francs	85.19 Francs
Germany	1.6950 Marks	25.43 Marks
Greece	291.88 Drachmas	4378.20 Drachmas
Ireland	0.6767 Punt	10.15 Punts
Italy	1673.00 Lira	25,095.00 Lira
Netherlands	1.9100 Guilders	28.65 Guilders
Portugal	173.70 Escudos	2605.50 Escudos
Spain	143.94 Pesetas	2159.10 Pesetas

(Source: Wall Street Journal)

2. 3500 lira is about $2.09 U.S.

3. $15.00 U.S. is equal to 12.93 ECU (rounded to the nearest hundredth).

$$\frac{\$1.1601}{\$15.00} = \frac{1 \text{ ECU}}{12.93 \text{ ECU}}$$

EXTENSIONS

• Find the current rates of exchange for these countries and recalculate the information in the chart. The current rate of exchange is usually listed in major newspapers or is available at local banks.

• Search the Internet for national prices of a known commodity, such as soda or blue jeans. Determine in which country you could purchase the commodity for the fewest U. S. dollars.

▶ Euro Dollar, I'm a Currency

**References to
MATH ON CALL**

Guinevere and her family are on a trip in Europe. As they travel to each new country, they have to exchange money, since each European country has its own monetary system. Soon, Guinevere and her family realize they are forever exchanging money.

Guinevere promised her grandmother, who loves chocolate, that she would buy her some chocolate in every country the family visited. Guinevere's parents have allotted her $15.00 in United States currency to spend for chocolate in each country. Guinevere has set up a chart to make it easier to see how much she can spend for chocolate in each country.

1. Complete the chart. Round answers to the nearest hundredth.

Country Visited	$1.00 U.S. equals:	$15.00 U.S. equals:
Belgium	34.900 Francs	523.50 Francs
France	5.6790 Francs	
Germany	1.6950 Marks	
Greece	291.88 Drachmas	
Ireland	0.6767 Punt	
Italy	1673.00 Lira	
Netherlands	1.9100 Guilders	
Portugal	173.70 Escudos	
Spain	143.94 Pesetas	

(Source: Wall Street Journal)

2. Guinevere finds a box of chocolate in Italy marked 3500 lira. How much is that in U.S. dollars?

_____

After arriving in Europe, Guinevere discovers a new currency called the European Currency Unit (ECU). This is money that is accepted in all participating European countries. Guinevere finds out that $1.1601 U.S. is equal to 1 ECU.

3. What is the ECU equivalent value of $15.00 U.S.?

_____

Just Give Me a Call . . .

30–45 minutes

OBJECTIVES

- Compare prices on long-term investments
- Calculate costs of pagers over time
- Complete a table
- Analyze data in a table
- Define a function
- Develop a rule

MATERIALS

- calculators
- Quarter-Inch Grid Paper, page 120
- Pager Page, page 118

Computation

TEACHER NOTES

- A numeric pager relays only numeric messages. An alpha-numeric pager relays both letters and numbers. Discuss the need for different types of information. For example, if a doctor gets a page, is a telephone number alone going to be enough information?

- Discuss related vocabulary such as *airtime, activation fee, protection coverage, additional pagers* and *unlimited pagers.*

EXTENSIONS

- Discuss slope and constants, linear equations and functions. Determine the slope and intercept of this function.

- Research how pager systems work. How do pagers affect the need for new area codes?

ANSWERS

2. Numeric Pager: Cool Communiqués; Alpha-Numeric Pager: Fetch-A-Friend

3. No

4. Fetch-A-Friend

5. Cool Communiqués

6. Check the graphs made by the students. The axes should be labeled "total cost" and "months." The points to be plotted are given in the completed tables. Check for accuracy and the use of an appropriate scale. The points should not be connected with lines, since this is a graph of a discrete function.

7. Independent variable = number of months

8. Dependent variable = cost

9. This is a discrete function. Since the time period stated in each company's terms is the month, it is not possible to pay for partial months (days).

1.

Numeric Pagers	Cool Communiqués		Fetch-A-Friend	
	Function: $13.00m	Total cost	Function: $39.00 + $15.00 + $8.95m	Total cost
1 month	$13.00	$13.00	$54.00 + $8.95	$62.95
3 months	$13.00(3)	$39.00	$54.00 + $8.95(3)	$80.85
6 months	$13.00(6)	$78.00	$54.00 + $8.95(6)	$107.70
9 months	$13.00(9)	$117.00	$54.00 + $8.95(9)	$134.55
12 months	$13.00(12)	$156.00	$54.00 + $8.95(12)	$161.40
15 months	$13.00(15)	$195.00	$54.00 + $8.95(15)	$188.25
n months	13.00n$	13.00n$	$54.00 + 8.95n$	$54.00 + 8.95n$

Alpha-Numeric Pagers	Cool Communiqués		Fetch-A-Friend	
	Function: $30.00m	Total cost	Function: $49.00 + $15.00 + $13.95m	Total cost
1 month	$30.00	$30.00	$49.00 + $15.00 + $13.95	$77.95
3 months	$30.00(3)	$90.00	$49.00 + $15.00 + $13.95	$105.85
6 months	$30.00(6)	$180.00	$49.00 + $15.00 + $13.95	$147.70
9 months	$30.00(9)	$270.00	$49.00 + $15.00 + $13.95	$189.55
12 months	$30.00(12)	$360.00	$49.00 + $15.00 + $13.95	$231.40
15 months	$30.00(15)	$450.00	$49.00 + $15.00 + $13.95	$273.25
n months	30.00n$	30.00n$	$49.00 + $15.00 + $13.95	$64.00 + 13.95n$

Name _____

▶ Just Give Me a Call . . .

References to MATH ON CALL

Pagers have become a popular communication tool. Customers want many options at a minimal cost. Below are two options for pagers and service. Each company has both a numeric pager (numbers only) and an alpha-numeric pager (numbers and letters).

BEEP

Company	Pager type	Pager cost	Monthly airtime fee	Activation fee
Cool Communiqués	Numeric	free	$13.00	none
	Alpha-Numeric	free	$30.00	none
Fetch-A-Friend	Numeric	$39.00	$8.95	$15.00
	Alpha-Numeric	$49.00	$13.95	$15.00

1. Complete the tables on the Pager Page and determine the function for each company, for numeric and alpha-numeric pagers.

2. What are the best choices for six months of numeric and alpha-numeric paging services?

_____

3. If you were considering keeping the pager for 1 year, would that change your choice? _____

4. If this is a three-year investment, which company would you choose?

_____

5. Your mom gives you a pager so she can always find you this summer. What company provides the best price for 3 months? _____

6. Use your grid paper to graph the costs of each pager for the time periods listed. Make one graph to compare numeric pagers and another graph to compare alpha-numeric pagers.

7. Which is the independent variable? _____

8. Which is the dependent variable? _____

9. Is this function discrete or continuous? _____

Algebra

Is It a Real Deal?

30–45 minutes

OBJECTIVES

- Use a verbal model to solve a real-life problem.
- Write mathematical expressions

MATERIALS

- newspapers (optional)

TEACHER NOTES

- In this activity students use real-life information to solve a problem.

- Students create verbal models to represent real-life information and use the verbal models to answer questions. They also use the answers from these questions to make consumer decisions.

- Knowing how to create verbal models of real-life situations will help students make informed consumer decisions.

EXTENSIONS

- Ask students to choose something they would like to purchase. Provide students with newspapers to look for ads.

- Ask students to write verbal models for the ads they find in the newspaper.

ANSWERS

1. (Cost of less than 12 lessons) equals $22.50 times (the number of lessons)

   Cost = $22.50x$

2. (Cost of 12 or more lessons) equals $180 plus $22.50 times (the total number of lessons minus 12)

   Cost = $180 + 22.50(x - 12)$

3. $247.50

4. (Cost of lessons) equals $18 times (the number of lessons minus 3)

   Cost = $18(x - 3)$

5. $216

6. $270

7. Used guitar from Johnny's World of Music: $140

   Guitar lessons from the classifieds: $247.50

8. Total cost = $387.50

▶ **Is It a Real Deal?**

Variables and
    Constants: **202**

Expressions and
    Equations: **203**

Writing Algebraic
    Expressions: **204**

Find Needed
    Information: **490**

**References to
MATH ON CALL**

You want to buy a guitar and take 15 lessons. To do this spending the least amount of money, you check the newspaper ads for prices on new guitars, used guitars, and guitar lessons. Some ads are shown below.

1. Use the information in the classifieds to write a verbal model and a mathematical expression that represent the cost of taking less than 12 lessons.

    _____

    _____

2. Use the information in the classifieds to write a verbal model and a mathematical expression that represent the cost of 12 or more lessons.

    _____

    _____

Classified

Private Guitar Lessons:
    $22.50 a lesson.
Special: 12 lessons for
    $180, save $90!!!

Used Guitar For Sale:
    Good condition.
    Great Deal! Only $175.

---

3. From the information in the classifieds, how much would 15 private

    lessons cost? _____

4. Write a verbal model and a mathematical expression that represent the cost of 15 lessons at Johnny's World of Music, if you buy a new guitar.

    _____

    _____

Johnny's World of Music

New guitars* for $250
Used guitars for $140
Guitar lessons for
    $18.00 a lesson

* 3 free lessons with the
    purchase of a new
    guitar!!!!

---

5. How much would 15 lessons cost at Johnny's World of Music, if you

    bought a new guitar? _____

6. How much would 15 lessons cost at Johnny's World of Music, if you

    did not buy a new guitar? _____

7. To spend the least amount of money, which guitar should you buy and where should you take your 15 guitar lessons?

    _____

    _____

8. How much will it cost? _____

Look Out Below!

45–60 minutes

OBJECTIVES

- Create and record expressions
- Use knowledge and understanding of order of operations.

MATERIALS

- three 1–6 number cubes per group
- a copy of the game board on page 123 for each group
- one game piece per student
- a Math Notebook Page, page 119, for each student

TEACHER NOTES

- It is important that students record the expressions they create during this game. This allows the other students to verify the value of each expression. It also gives you an opportunity for assessment. Students frequently forget that multiplication and division are done in order from left to right before addition and subtraction.

EXTENSIONS

- Have students refer to *Math on Call* item number 209, and call attention to what the robot is saying. Create a new class phrase to help everyone remember the rules for order of operations.

- Have students write a story that contains a mathematical problem where the order of operations is important. The story might explain what happens when the operations are performed in the wrong order. Students can write and illustrate the story using some construction paper that has been folded and cut into book form.

- Have students write a word problem to go with an equation. The problem should require the use of operations in a specific order.

- For a variation of the game, use both positive and negative numbers on the cubes for practice with integer operations. Students will then be moving in both directions (up and down) on the game board.

ANSWERS

1. F
2. A
3. D
4. C
5. E
6. B

When playing the game, answers will vary. Strategy also plays a role. For example, if a student rolls a 2, 3, and 6, possible results are $2 \times 6 - 3 = 9$, $6 \div 3 + 2 = 4$, or $2 \times 3 + 6 = 12$. Using $(2 + 3) \times 6 = 30$ however, allows the player to move to 30 and "climb" the ladder to 50.

Algebra

▶ **Look Out Below!**

**References to
MATH ON CALL**

Read this list of events in a typical student's life and put them in sequential order with the first event happening about 7 A.M. Write the appropriate letter to the right of the numbers at the right so that all items are in order.

A Leave for school   I. _____

B Have dinner   2. _____

C Eat lunch   3. _____

D Arrive at school   4. _____

E Leave school   5. _____

F Wake up   6. _____

Order is very important in the world around us, and it is just as important in mathematics. The game you are about to play will challenge your ability to use order of operations.

HOW TO PLAY THE GAME:

a. Make a group of 2–4 players. You will need three 1–6 number cubes and a copy of the game board for your group. Each player needs a Math Notebook Page and a game piece, such as a colored paper clip.

b. The person whose birthday is closest to the start of the school year goes first, and begins by rolling the three cubes. Using the numbers on the cubes and any mathematical operation ($+$, $-$, $\times$, or $\div$) only once, the player creates an expression that can be simplified to a whole number. For example, if a 2, 4, and 5 are rolled, possible expressions are $2 + 4 - 5$ which equals 1, or $4 \times 5 - 2$ which equals 18. The whole number value of the expression is the number of spaces the player moves forward. If the player is unable to create an expression, that player forfeits his or her turn.

c. Players must record their expressions using appropriate mathematical notation on their Math Notebook Page.

d. Other players may challenge the answer. If the challenged answer is correct, the player gets to take a second turn. If the answer is incorrect, the player loses the current turn.

e. Play then passes to the next person on the left. The process repeats.

f. If you land on a number that has a slide attached, you must go down the slide. If you land on a square that has an attached ladder, you can go up the ladder.

g. To win, a player must reach 100 or more. The winner can parachute down to a soft landing on the big pillow!

Step Right Up

OBJECTIVES

- Analyze data to determine slope
- Use data from a table to graph a linear equation

MATERIALS

TEACHER NOTES

- This activity uses the stairs of the Empire State Building to show how the concept of slope is used in the world around us. The reminder about rounding in question 2 is important. Use it to help students realize what happens when mathematical concepts are applied in the real world. Remember that a flight of stairs is not needed for each floor, since the 102nd floor is the top floor.

- The table that students complete gives them the coordinate pairs they need to make the graph. Talk about how the graph is to be made and plot a few points with the students. The resulting points are shown for you on the graph below. Discuss the slope of a line.

ANSWERS

1. Twelve feet

2. Eighteen steps

3. Eight inches

4. See the points on the line in the graph below.

5.

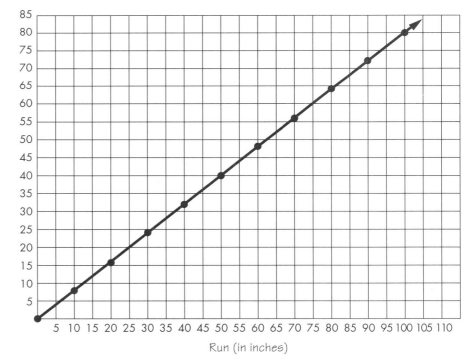

Rise (in inches)

Run (in inches)

6. The slope of the line is $\frac{\text{rise}}{\text{run}} = \frac{8}{10} = \frac{4}{5}$.

▶ Step Right Up

**References to
MATH ON CALL**

The Empire State Building in New York City was built at the rate of $4\frac{1}{2}$ stories each week. The building has 102 floors. The height from street level to the top of the 102nd floor is 1224 feet. There are 1860 steps.

1. For the purposes of this exercise, we will assume that all floors are the same height. What is the height of each floor? _____

2. How many steps are between each floor? Remember that fractional parts of steps make no sense in this case, so round your answer to the nearest whole step. _____

3. What is the height of each step in inches? _____

The height of a step is actually called the *rise* and the depth is called the tread or *run*. Standard building codes list the required rise of a step as 8 inches and the required run as 10 inches.

4. Complete the table to the left to determine how many inches you go up and across for each of the first ten steps.

5. Plot the rise and run of the first ten steps on the graph provided.

	run	rise
floor	0	0
1 step	10"	8"
2 steps	20"	16"
3 steps		
4 steps		
5 steps		
6 steps		
7 steps		
8 steps		
9 steps		
10 steps		

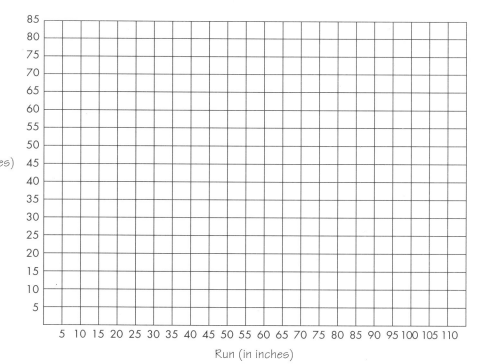

Rise
(in inches)

Run (in inches)

6. What is the slope of this line? _____

Sticky π

OBJECTIVE

• Graph the lengths of the diameter and circumference to develop π as a ratio for slope

MATERIALS

• assorted circular jar lids
• large one-inch graph paper (This can be purchased on a roll or a flip chart.)
• masking tape
• dry spaghetti
• straightedge or ruler

45–60 minutes

TEACHER NOTES

• In this activity students will discover the relationship between a circle's diameter and circumference.

• A circle's circumference has a direct relationship to its diameter. The relationship is a linear function where the diameter is the independent variable and the circumference is the dependent variable. The relationship can be represented by the linear function $C = \pi d$, where C is the circumference and d is the diameter.

• The ratio of the dependent variable to the independent variable is C/d.

• By measuring the diameters and circumferences of several different circles, the students will discover that the relationship can be defined by the constant π.

EXTENSIONS

• Students can use a graphing calculator to plot the diameter and circumference of several circles.

• Have students use a graphing calculator to graph the function $y = \pi x$. Point out that when the function $y = \pi x$ is graphed, the line extends into the third quadrant. While the function can have negative values, these values are meaningless when we talk about the diameter and circumference of a circle.

ANSWERS

1–3. Answers will vary. The student's graph should resemble the graph shown here.

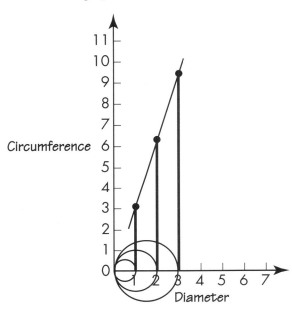

4. The tape measures about 3.14 units.

5. The length of the tape for all circles is about the same.

6. The vertical line measures about 3.14 units.

7. The length of the vertical unit is about 3.14 times the length of the horizontal unit.

▶ Sticky π

**References to
MATH ON CALL**

1. On large graph paper, draw the first quadrant of a coordinate grid. (See graph below.) Label the horizontal axis "Diameter." Label the vertical axis "Circumference."

2. Your teacher will give you several jar lids of different sizes. For each lid, complete the following four steps. Begin with the smallest lid.

   a. Place the lid over the horizontal axis of your coordinate grid so that the left edge of the lid is at the origin.

   b. Trace the lid on the grid paper and mark the diameter of the lid along the horizontal axis.

   c. Measure the circumference of the lid by placing masking tape around the edge of the lid. Cut the tape to the exact circumference and remove it from the lid.

   d. Place the tape on the grid paper so that:
   • The length of the tape is parallel to the vertical axis.
   • The left edge of the tape meets the corresponding diameter that you marked on the horizontal axis.
   • The bottom edge of the tape is on the horizontal axis.

3. With your pencil, place a dot on the upper left corner of each piece of masking tape. Using a straightedge, draw a line through the dots.

4. Break a piece of spaghetti into the length of the diameter of the smallest circle. This length represents one unit measure. Using this piece of spaghetti, measure the length of the masking tape corresponding to the smallest circle. How many units long is the tape?

_____

5. Repeat step 4 using two other circles from your graph with each unit of measure being the diameter of the circle. Is the length of the tape

about the same or different for each circle? _____

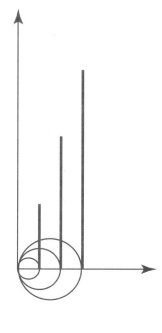

6. Use another piece of spaghetti to measure from the dot on one piece of masking tape horizontally to the left edge of the next piece of tape. Break the spaghetti into this length. This length represents one unit measure. Next, place the spaghetti over the horizontal axis of your graph so that one end of the spaghetti is at the origin. Mark the point where the spaghetti ends. Then draw a vertical line from that point to the line that you drew in step 3 to connect the dots. Finally, measure the vertical line using your spaghetti unit. How long is the

vertical line? _____

7. Each time you compare the vertical unit to the horizontal unit, what

do you find? _____

Triple Play

OBJECTIVE
• Generate Pythagorean Triples

MATERIALS
• construction paper
• calculators (optional)

30–45 minutes

TEACHER NOTES

• You may want to have students construct this proof of the Pythagorean Theorem.

Directions: Measure and cut out four congruent triangles whose legs have the lengths a and b and a square whose side is $a + b$. Move the four triangles to see that the squares of the two legs take up the same area as the square of the hypotenuse.

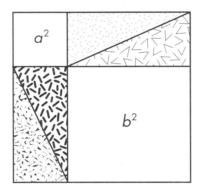

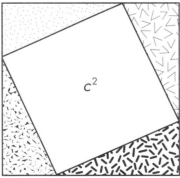

EXTENSIONS

• Primitive triples are triples that have no common factors. The sets 3, 4, 5 and 5, 12, 13 are primitive triples. Have students determine the special rules required to generate primitive triples. (To generate primitive triples students must start with relatively prime values for u and v which are even and odd.)

• Have students create a spreadsheet or a program in a graphing calculator to generate triples.

• Have students use 1 cm Grid Paper and 1 cm cubes to build squares on the three sides of a right triangle to verify the Pythagorean Theorem.

ANSWERS

1. 9, 8
2. 81, 64
3. $81 - 64 =$ **17**
4. $2 \times 8 \times 9 =$ **144**
5. $81 + 64 =$ **145**
6. **17, 144, 145**
7. Test: $17^2 + 144^2 = 145^2$
   $289 + 20{,}736 = 21{,}025$
8. u, v
9. u^2, v^2
10. $u^2 - v^2$
11. $2uv$
12. $u^2 + v^2$

13–15. Answers will vary according to the numbers chosen by students.

16.

Pythagorean Triple	u	v
3, 4, 5	2	1
5, 12, 13	3	2

▶ Triple Play

Evaluating Algebraic
Expressions: **206**

Order of Operations: **207**

Rules for Order of
Operations: **209**

Pythagorean Theorem: **359**

**References to
MATH ON CALL**

In item number 359, *Math on Call* mentions two sets of whole numbers
that represent measures of sides of a right triangle—the 3-4-5 and 5-12-
13 right triangles. These sets are called Pythagorean Triples. To generate
a set of Pythagorean Triples, follow these steps.

Try this using 9 and 8.

a. Choose any two numbers. $(5, 3)$ **1.** _____

b. Square each number. $(25, 9)$ **2.** _____

c. Find the difference of the squares.   **3.** _____
$(25 - 9 = \underline{\mathbf{16}})$

d. Double the product of the original   **4.** _____
numbers. $(2 \times 5 \times 3 = \underline{\mathbf{30}})$

e. Find the sum of the squares. $(25 + 9 = \underline{\mathbf{34}})$ **5.** _____

f. The results of steps (**c**), (**d**), and (**e**)   **6.** _____
create a Pythagorean Triple. $(\underline{\mathbf{16}}, \underline{\mathbf{30}}, \underline{\mathbf{34}})$

g. Test: $16^2 + 30^2 = 34^2$ **7.** Test: _____

$256 + 900 = 1156$ _____

Now write the steps using algebra. Let u and v represent two different
whole numbers. Let the larger value be u. Let the smaller value be v.

8. Choose any two numbers. _____   **9.** Square each number. _____

10. Find the difference of the squares. _____

11. Double the product of the original numbers. _____

12. Find the sum of the squares. _____

Choose three pairs of numbers. For each pair, use the expressions you
created in steps 8–12 to create a set of Pythagorean Triples.

13. Numbers: ____, ____   Pythagorean Triple ____, ____, ____

14. Numbers: ____, ____   Pythagorean Triple ____, ____, ____

15. Numbers: ____, ____   Pythagorean Triple ____, ____, ____

Pythagorean Triple	u	v
3, 4, 5		
5, 12, 13		

16. In the table to the left, write the values
for u and v that make each of these
Pythagorean Triples.

30–45 minutes

Just Another Dimension

Algebra

OBJECTIVE

- Analyze common elements in formulas and understand their relationship

MATERIALS

- Math Notebook Page, page 119

TEACHER NOTES

- Quite often students use formulas without understanding how the formula was derived. In this activity, students will see the similarity of formulas for 2- and 3-dimensional figures and realize the main difference is the addition of the third dimension. Students should also notice the relationship between volume and area as well as the relationship between circumference and surface area.

- A ream of paper can be used to illustrate volume. One sheet of paper alone is a good model for area. Layer 500 sheets together to create a 3-dimensional prism, a good model for volume.

EXTENSION

- Look through the other formulas in the Glossary of Mathematical Formulas in *Math on Call* with the students. Have them find two different formulas that have common elements. Work with them to list the formulas, what they are used for, and why they think they have the common elements.

ANSWERS

1. area of a triangle $A = \frac{1}{2}bh$
   area of a parallelogram $A = bh$

   These formulas have bh in common. The area of a triangle is half the area of a parallelogram with the same base and height.

2. area of a square $A = s^2$
   volume of a cube $V = s^3$

   These formulas have s^3 in common; $s^3 = s^2 \times s$. To find the volume of a cube, multiply the area of the base (s^2) by the height of the cube (s).

3. circumference of a circle $C = 2\pi r$
   lateral surface area of a cylinder $S = 2\pi rh$

   These formulas have $2\pi r$ in common. The lateral surface of a cylinder is a rectangle with length equal to the circumference of the base ($2\pi r$) and width equal to the height of the cylinder (h).

4. area of a rectangle $A = lw$
   volume of a rectangular prism $V = lwh$

   These formulas have lw in common. To find the volume of a rectangular prism, multiply the area of the base (lw) by the height of the rectangular prism (h).

5. area of a circle $A = \pi r^2$
   volume of a cylinder $V = \pi r^2 h$

   These formulas have πr^2 in common. To find the volume of a cylinder, multiply the area of the circular base (πr^2) by the height of the cylinder (h).

6. volume of a cylinder $V = \pi r^2 h$
   volume of a cone $V = \frac{1}{3}\pi r^2 h$

   These formulas have $\pi r^2 h$ in common. The volume of a cone is $\frac{1}{3}$ the volume of a cylinder with the same base.

7. Students should understand that, for a square, squaring the sides (s^2) gives the same result as multiplying the length and width (lw) of a rectangle, since all squares are rectangles. In both cases, the new formula results from adding a third dimension.

► Just Another Dimension

Area of Triangles: **356**

Area of Parallelograms: **367**

Look for Patterns: **484**

Glossary of Mathematical Formulas: **560–566**

References to MATH ON CALL

Lynn is sitting in Ms. Cheng's math class. Ms. Cheng is demonstrating the use of formulas to quickly arrive at answers. Lynn is trying to substitute the numbers from sketches into the formulas, but does not see any connection. Complete the questions below and help Lynn understand the common elements in formulas.

List the formulas, highlight common elements, and write why you think the formulas are similar for each problem below. Use your Math Notebook Page if you need more space for your answers.

1. area of a triangle $A = \frac{1}{2}bh$ _____

   area of a parallelogram $A = bh$ _____

2. area of a square   _____   _____

   volume of a cube   _____   _____

3. circumference of
   a circle   _____   _____

   surface area of
   a cylinder   _____   _____

4. area of a rectangle   _____   _____

   volume of a
   rectangular prism   _____   _____

5. area of a circle   _____   _____

   volume of a cylinder   _____   _____

6. volume of a cylinder   _____   _____

   volume of a cone   _____   _____

7. Compare the answers from questions 2 and 4. What common elements do they share? Why?

   _____

   _____

   _____

   _____

Algebra

How Much Fun?

45–60 minutes

OBJECTIVES

- Complete a table of data
- Write an equation from the table
- Use a graph to solve a system of equations
- Determine which variables are independent and dependent

MATERIALS

- 1 cm Grid Paper, page 121
- calculators (optional)

TEACHER NOTES

- Students will need to spend time studying the table and discussing the information.

- Real amusement parks do not all structure their admission prices in the same way. For example, some parks define children by age and others by height.

- Students should select the appropriate ticket (adult or child) for the amusement park they choose. While middle-school students will probably all be more than 11 years old, some may be less than 4 feet tall.

EXTENSIONS

- The criteria for what constitutes a child varies from park to park. Do students think it's fair that a 14-year-old who is less than 4 feet tall can get into Funtown USA as a child? How does this relate to height requirements on rides?

- Give students this scenario about a day at an amusement park. A person arrives at the park when it opens at 10:00 A.M. and pays $30.00 including parking to get in. He or she must leave at 5:30 P.M. to get to work on time. Between 10:00 and 11:00 A.M. he or she has gone on 2 rides. After 11:00 A.M., the park is more crowded and there is a two hour wait for each ride. How much does each ride cost?

- Have students plan a week-long trip to an amusement park. Use travel brochures or other sources to determine costs of transportation, lodging, and meals as well as the cost of admission to the amusement park. You can also set up a budget for the trip.

- Have students create a graph showing the change in cost per visit using a Season Pass good for up to 10 trips to the park. What will the graph look like? For example, if the Season Pass costs $75.00, then on the second visit the cost will be $37.50, the third visit will cost $25.00, and so on.

ANSWERS

1. Answers will vary.

2. n times the 1-Day Admission price

3. Season Pass price divided by n

4. Graphs will vary according to the park chosen by each student. Check student work.

5. The number of visits is the independent variable.

6. The cost per visit is the dependent variable.

▶ How Much Fun?

The table below shows admission prices for six different imaginary amusement parks. Select an amusement park. Determine how many times you would have to go to the park at the 1-Day Admission price before it would be more economical to buy the Season Pass. Remember to include the cost of parking every day. The Season Pass prices include parking charges.

Use this table to organize your data.

Relations and Functions: 232–236

Writing Equations from Tables of Values: 244

Graphing Equations: 245

Using a Table to Graph a Linear Equation: 247

Using a Graph to Solve a System of Equations: 255

References to MATH ON CALL

Park:		
	1-Day Admission	Season Pass
1 visit		
2 visits		
3 visits		
4 visits		
n visits		

1. How many visits at the 1-Day Admission rate will it take before you save money by buying a Season Pass? _____

2. Write an equation for the cost of n visits to the park at the 1-Day Admission price. _____

3. Write an equation for the cost of n visits to the park at the Season Pass rate. _____

4. Use the data in the table above and your grid paper to make a double-line graph. One line will show the 1-Day Admission rate for multiple visits. The other line will show the Season Pass rate for multiple visits. Read about dependent and independent variables in *Math on Call* to determine how to label and structure the axes on your graph.

5. Which is the independent variable? _____

6. Which is the dependent variable? _____

Amusement Park Prices:				
1-Day Admission:	Adult	Child	Parking	Season Pass
Funtown USA	$31.95	$20.95 (under 48 inches tall)	$5.00	$74.95
Coaster City	$34.00	$29.00 (4–10 years old)	$7.00	$110.35
Play Land	$29.95	$24.95 (4–10 years old)	$20.00	$74.95
Rides Galore!	$32.00	$22.50 (under 48 inches tall)	$5.00	$89.95
Thrill Park	$38.00	$28.00 (3–11 years old)	$30.00	$99.00
Crash & Carry	$42.00	$34.00 (3–9 years old)	free	$299.00

Your Result Is Debatable

OBJECTIVES

- Understand how data is arranged in a chart
- Analyze and evaluate data
- Analyze interpretations of collected data for accuracy

MATERIALS

20–30 minutes

TEACHER NOTES

- This activity is designed to allow the students to interpret data and statistics and to evaluate statements related to the data. The word choices of the statements are intentionally broad to allow for discussion and different interpretations.

EXTENSIONS

- Write five additional statements based on this data. Decide if they are true or false.

- Students can design an opinion poll and use a random sample of students in the school population for data. Have students include at least 10% of the school population as a sample. Work with the students to develop a method for determining who to include in the survey so that the group is representative of the entire school population. See *Math on Call* item number 267 for some helpful guidelines. The results of the survey can be published in the school newspaper.

ANSWERS

1. True. Fifteen of the 20 responses (75%) express disagreement with the proposal for school uniforms. Using the word "opposed" for the students who disagree is an interpretation for discussion.

2. True. Thirteen responses in agreement with the proposal represents a majority. Again, use of the word "desire" is an interpretation that is open for discussion.

3. True. The difference between those that agreed and those that disagreed is small.

4. True. Because the statement uses the same words as the original survey question, there is no need for discussion about the interpretation of the responses in this case.

5. True. Only one student (5%) had no opinion on this question.

6. False. The statement tries to draw a conclusion about the opinion of the entire student body, and there is no way to know if the members of the debating club make up a good random sample of the entire student population. While the statement is true about members of the debating club, it may not be a good generalization for all the students in the school.

▶ Your Result Is Debatable

Taking Samples: **264**

Recording Data: **268**

Arranging Data: **271**

**References to
MATH ON CALL**

Initial results from the survey of 20 debating club members at one school revealed the following information.

The State Debating Organization has created a survey to be used in the upcoming competition. Each local school debating club must survey its own student body, report accurate statistics, and summarize the information. The survey is shown below.

For each statement, students should say whether they strongly agree, agree, have no opinion, disagree, or strongly disagree.

1. Students should wear uniforms in school.
2. Students should be grouped into same-sex classes for academics.
3. Students should be allowed to leave campus for lunch.
4. Students should be allowed to carry radios with headphones.
5. School officials should be allowed to conduct locker searches.

Question	Strongly Agree	Agree	No Opinion	Disagree	Strongly Disagree
#1	2	2	1	12	3
#2	4	5	4	3	4
#3	11	2	4	1	2
#4	6	5	0	6	3
#5	5	4	1	6	4

Decide if the following statements are true or false based on these results and tell why.

1. 75% of the members surveyed are opposed to school uniforms.

_____

2. The majority of members desire an open campus for lunch.

_____

3. There was no clear majority opinion about grouping classes by sex.

_____

4. More than half of the members agreed that students should be allowed to carry radios if desired.

_____

5. 95% of the debating club members had opinions about locker searches.

_____

6. Less than half of the entire student body would object to same-sex

classes. _____

Looks Are Deceiving

OBJECTIVES

- Determine how a graph can be deceiving
- Make a bar graph
- Make a circle graph

MATERIALS

- 1 cm Grid Paper, page 121

30–45 minutes

TEACHER NOTES

- Many companies take data and create graphs presenting the data the way they want it to be interpreted. Upon close examination, discrepancies in the graph or the type of graph chosen may mislead the reader. This activity will make students aware of such a deception. After the students realize that the marks on the vertical axis are first counted by 5 and then by 2, they must re-graph the data appropriately.

EXTENSIONS

- Students can look through newspapers for graphs. Have them select several graphs and determine if they are deceptive or not. They can write a paragraph about their conclusions.

- Have students take a non-deceptive graph and find a way to present the information in a misleading manner by incorporating a deceptive practice.

ANSWERS

1. The scale on the vertical axis of the graph changes as it goes up, even though the spacing between marks does not change. First the marks are by 5, then by 2.

2.

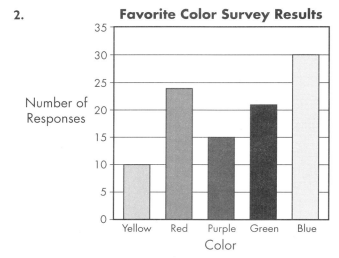

Favorite Color Survey Results

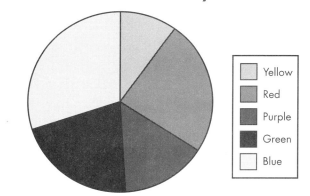

Favorite Color Survey Results

3. The bar graph shows the *number of people* who chose each color.

4. The circle graph shows *what part of the whole group* chose each color.

5. Answers will vary.

▶ **Looks Are Deceiving**

**References to
MATH ON CALL**

A survey of 100 people was conducted. Each was asked to tell her or his favorite color. The data collected is shown in the graph. Study the graph carefully.

1. What is wrong with the graph?

_____

_____

_____

_____

_____

_____

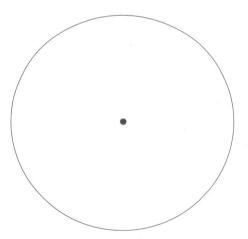

Favorite Color Survey Results

Number of Responses

Color

Yellow Red Purple Green Blue

2. Use the data above to construct both a bar graph and a circle graph correctly. Use your grid paper for the bar graph. Use this circle for the circle graph.

3. What information is shown on the bar graph but not on the circle

graph? _____

4. What information is shown on the circle graph but not on the bar

graph? _____

5. Tell which graph you would use when writing a report about the.

survey and explain why. _____

_____

Graphs and Statistics

Put Your Best Graph Forward

OBJECTIVE
• Determine the best graph to use for displaying various sets of data

MATERIALS
none

20–30 minutes

TEACHER NOTES

• Bar graphs, pictographs, and histograms are graphs that compare categories and numbers. Generally, one axis is numeric and the other is not.

• Circle graphs compare parts as they relate to the whole. Students should choose this kind of graph when a total group is separated into different sections, parts, or regions.

• Line graphs are best at showing change over time. Emphasize that time is continuous, but quantitative information is marked at measurable points for comparison. One axis shows a measure of time and the other shows a numeric quantity.

• Line plots, box-and-whisker plots, stem-and-leaf plots, and scatter plots are graphs that show how data are clustered. They are best used when numbers within a single category are to be compared. For example, if there are two axes, as in a scatter plot, each axis is labeled with numeric values. One axis might be labeled with the number of items purchased and the other axis labeled with the cost of the items.

EXTENSION

• Have students collect data graphs from sources such as newspapers, magazines, and so on. Students should try to find examples of each type of graph. These can then be analyzed for their appropriateness in displaying the collected data.

ANSWERS

1–8. See table below.

9. Answers will vary. Discuss the ideas students suggest and what may be the best way to present their information. Students can actually complete surveys and graph the results. Topics might include the changing value of gold over the last 50 years, favorite hobbies of all sixth-graders in the school, total time spent on homework by classmates, and so on.

	Data	Clues	Type of Graph
Ex.	prices of cars	span of years (time)	line graph
1.	test scores	median and individual scores	box-and-whisker plot
2.	breeds of dogs	number of different breeds	circle graph
3.	annual salaries	comparisons: men and women/5 careers	double-line graph
4.	river levels	span of months (time)	line graph
5.	number of parks	in the U.S. by region	circle graph
6.	length of telephone calls	number of minutes	line plot
7.	total sales	5 different CDs	bar graph
8.	average allowance	span of years (time)	line graph

▶ Put Your Best Graph Forward

Graphs are great communicators of information. However, it is important to choose the best type of graph to display the collected information. Often clue words in the description of the data help you decide which graph will work best to show the information you have. *Math on Call* identifies three large categories of graphs and gives some guidelines for their use. Identify which is the most appropriate graph to display the following sets of data.

Complete the chart, describing the data, any clues, and the type of graph.

Example: the average price of a new car between 1920 and 1990

Graphs that Compare:
   291–296

Graphs That Show Change Over Time:
   297–299

Graphs That Show How Data Are Clustered:
   300–305

References to MATH ON CALL

1. median test score and scores for each member of the class

2. different breeds of dogs in the local dog show and number of each breed

3. comparison of annual salaries of men and women in five different careers

4. water level of the Mississippi River over the past calendar year

5. number of national parks in the United States by region

6. length in minutes of telephone calls by teenagers

7. total national sales of five different CDs

8. average allowance of 14-year-olds over the past 50 years

	Data	Clues	Type of Graph
Ex.	prices of cars	span of years (time)	line graph
1.			
2.			
3.			
4.			
5.			
6.			
7.			
8.			

9. Choose two topics of your own for data-collecting. Determine which type of graph will work best to communicate the information you collect.

Unpredictable or Not?

45–60 minutes

OBJECTIVES

• Analyze data to determine correlations
• Construct a scatter plot

MATERIALS

• Quarter-Inch Grid Paper, page 120

TEACHER NOTES

• There is a direct correlation between the wind speed, barometric pressure, and the movement of a hurricane.

• Once a hurricane reaches landfall, the winds and pressure drop. The direction of the storm also modifies.

• In the Northern Hemisphere, hurricanes swirl clockwise.

• In general, the northeast side of a hurricane causes the most wind damage. The southwest side of the hurricane causes the most rainfall. The level of rainfall often rises after landfall.

EXTENSIONS

• Ask students to complete further research on severe weather and determine what types of storms are predictable.

• Investigate the webpage of the National Hurricane Tracking Center in Florida with the students. (*http://wxp.atms.purdue.edu/hurricane/*)

• Students can explore community plans for evacuation routes for the types of severe weather in your area. Then students can write a newspaper article using the information they found.

• Have students research the possible correlations between geographic phenomenon, such as an earthquake and a volcano.

ANSWERS

1. The hurricane was most intense between 04/11 and 04/17.

2. The wind speed increased gradually until it reached 85 mph at 9:00 P.M. on October 3. Then it quickly increased to 115 mph at 11:00 A.M. on October 4.

3.

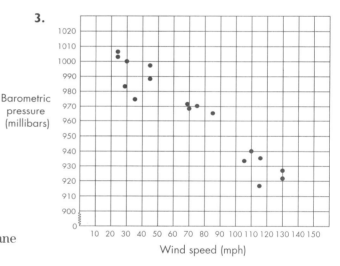

4. Yes. As the barometric pressure decreases, the wind speed increases.

▶ Unpredictable or Not?

References to MATH ON CALL

The data shown in the table below are from Hurricane Opal, which was tracked in 1995. The column labeled Day/Time shows the day in September or October and the time in military time. For example, 04/23 represents October 4 at 11:00 P.M.

Day/Time	Barometric Pressure (millibars)	Wind Speed (miles per hour)	Status
27/21	1005	25	Tropical Depression
28/21	1004	25	Tropical Depression
29/21	1000	30	Tropical Depression
30/21	997	45	Tropical Storm
01/21	989	45	Tropical Storm
02/21	971	70	Hurricane-1
03/21	968	70	Hurricane-1
03/21	965	85	Hurricane-2
04/09	933	105	Hurricane-3
04/11	916	115	Hurricane-4
04/13	921	130	Hurricane-4
04/15	927	130	Hurricane-4
04/17	934	115	Hurricane-4
04/19	940	110	Hurricane-3
04/23	940	110	Hurricane-3
05/03	970	75	Hurricane-1
05/09	975	35	Tropical Storm
05/15	982	30	Tropical Depression

1. A hurricane is said to "intensify" as its wind speed increases. During

which time period was Hurricane Opal most intense? _____

_____

2. Explain your answer. _____

_____

3. Use the table and grid paper to construct a scatter plot of the relationship between the hurricane's barometric pressure and its wind speed.

4. Does the scatter plot show a correlation? If so, describe the correlation.

_____

_____

Put Your Story Where Your Graph Is

OBJECTIVES

- Read a story and determine which graph best represents the data in the story

MATERIALS

45–60 minutes

TEACHER NOTES

- Have students read each story more than once. On the first reading they should get a general sense of the story. On the second reading, students should consider what information can be graphed and what is happening to the numbers. Then students can read a third time, draw a sketch, and compare the sketch to the graphs.

- Discuss what might cause the difference between graphs that show straight lines and angular changes of direction and graphs with curved lines and more fluid changes in direction.

EXTENSIONS

- Give students a new story and have them make a graph to go with it.

- Have students create their own stories with matching graphs.

ANSWERS

1. Graph **C** best represents this story. Students should notice that as Jamal moves at faster speeds, his pulse rate increases slowly and that there is a sudden increase when he is chased by the dog.

2. The best label for the x-axis is "Time."

3. The best label for the y-axis is "Pulse rate."

4. Graph **A** best represents this story. Students should notice that the graph shows each stop Amanda makes, the times when she is driving at a fairly constant speed, and that the straightness of the line represents the smooth acceleration and deceleration of her car.

5. The best label for the x-axis is "Time."

6. The best label for the y-axis is "Speed."

7. Answers will vary. If there is time, have students share their stories. Point out the variety of situations that can be represented by a single graph.

Graphs and Statistics

▶ **Put Your Story Where Your Graph Is**

Graphs That Show
   Change Over Time: **297**

Single-Line Graphs: **298**

**References to
MATH ON CALL**

Read the two stories and determine which graph pictured on the left best represents the information in each story.

Story #1

Jamal puts on his running shoes and takes his pulse. He then begins his stretching exercises. After 10 minutes, he starts the rest of his routine. Jamal starts off with a brisk walk for 3–5 minutes on the track in the park. Following this, he begins jogging. Jamal wants to maintain his pace for 20 minutes, but after 15 minutes a dog starts to chase him. Jamal runs even faster until the dog gives up trying to catch him. Then he pauses to catch his breath. He decides he is ready to warm down with a brisk walk for 5 minutes.

1. Which graph best represents the changes in

   Jamal's pulse rate? _____

2. What label would you use for

   the x-axis? _____

3. What label would you use

   for the y-axis? _____

A

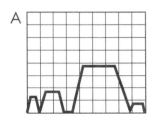

B

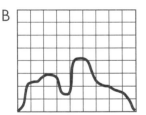

C

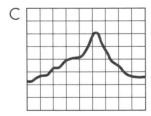

Story #2

Amanda is going shopping. She turns the key in the ignition of her car and the engine starts right up. She puts the car in gear and drives to the end of her street, where she stops. She has to wait for only one car. Then she turns right. She drives 2 miles and stops at a traffic light. When the light turns green, Amanda turns left and gets on the state highway where the speed limit is 55 miles per hour. After about 6 miles, she takes the exit for the mall. After stopping at the end of the exit ramp, she makes a right turn into the parking lot. She drives slowly to find a spot to park, pulls into a spot, and turns off her car.

4. Which graph best represents the changes in

   Amanda's speed? _____

5. What label would you use for the x-axis? _____

6. What label would you use for the y-axis? _____

7. Write a story for the graph not used. Tell how you would label the axes on the graph.

Graphs and Statistics

Funny Bones

OBJECTIVE
• Make a scatter plot

MATERIALS
• tape measure
• 1 cm Grid Paper, page 121

45–60 minutes

TEACHER NOTES

• Students will need to remove their shoes to get an accurate measurement for the leg.

• A discussion will need to take place on setting up the graph. Since it is difficult to distinguish between the dependent and independent variables in this instance, the labeling of the x- and y-axes is up to your discretion. The scale will need to be determined after considering the collected data.

EXTENSIONS

• Test the hypothesis presented in this activity with people of different ages.

• Are there any handicapping conditions that disprove the relationship developed in this activity?

• Compare the arm length to a person's height. Determine if there is any correlation.

ANSWERS

1. Check the graphs that students have made.

2. The line of best fit should approximate the diagonal (lower left corner to upper right corner) of the graph.

3. The length of a leg segment should be between 16 and 17 inches.

4. No. Although people of various ages and sizes can be measured, a measurement of 40 inches would be highly unlikely. It would mean that a person's lower leg is more than 3 feet long. Students rarely convert the measurements to determine if an answer is reasonable, but would be able to tell you that the typical person does not have a lower leg that is 3 feet long.

Name _____

▶ Funny Bones

1. Work with a partner to take the following measurements for each other. Record the measurements in the table. Then collect and record data from other student pairs until you have data from the entire class. Then plot the two sets of data as ordered pairs on your grid paper.

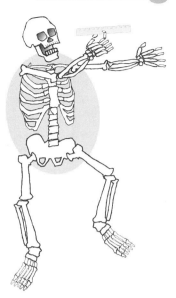

References to MATH ON CALL

Name	Length from inside bend of elbow to tip of fingers (in inches)	Length from bend at back of knee to floor (in inches)

This kind of graph is called a **scatter plot**. It is used to determine if pieces of data are related.

2. After graphing the data collected, draw a line of best fit on your scatter plot.

3. Predict the length of a leg segment for a person whose arm length is $15\frac{3}{4}$ inches. _____

4. Do you think it would be reasonable for a measurement of 40 inches to be recorded for the length of an arm segment? Why or why not?

_____

_____

_____

Sailing Circles

45–60 minutes

OBJECTIVES

• Understand triangulation
• Pinpoint a location using proportions

MATERIALS

• Sailing Circles Map, page 124
• compass

TEACHER NOTES

• The scenario on the student page gives the general idea of how triangulation works. It is more complicated than described, but the process is similar. Communication does take place between stations on the shoreline and boats. Loran stands for *long range navigation*. The loran system uses a time differential between electronic pulses to place a ship or aircraft on a chart. Readings between multiple stations are needed along with a special map that has loran coordinates.

• To locate the boat, students will measure and draw three circles that overlap. Once all three circles are drawn, the triangular area in the middle will show the location of the boat.

EXTENSIONS

• Have students research how and why a Cartesian Coordinate system was developed.

• Students can find out what navigational systems are used with airplanes. They can also research how radar systems work.

• Some cars are now equipped with GPS (Global Positioning System). Students can discover what this system is and how it works.

ANSWERS

1.

	Time it takes a signal to reach the boat	Distance from the boat to the station	Number of centimeters on the map
Station 1	20 seconds	50 miles	5
Station 2	18 seconds	45 miles	4.5
Station 3	32 seconds	80 miles	8

2. Check students work on the Sailing Circles Map. The triangle should be almost due east and a little south of Corpus Christi.

3. West

4. Between 50 and 60 miles

5. Three circles are needed to narrow the possible location of the boat. Two circles intersect at two points, giving the impression that the boat would be at exactly one of them. The boat could be anywhere in the area common to both circles. Using three circles reduces the size of the common area between the circles to the small triangular shape called the "crooked hat."

▶ Sailing Circles

**References to
MATH ON CALL**

Bryanna and Marquita decided to go offshore fishing one day. Around midday they noticed a storm brewing. It became a big enough storm to bounce them around and get them off course. Marquita was afraid that they were lost at sea. Bryanna told Marquita not to worry since she had a loran unit onboard. She went on to explain, "A loran unit helps pinpoint where we are. There are three stations on the shore that the unit communicates with. I send an electronic signal to each station. Each station sends a signal back. For every two seconds it takes for the signal to get back, I know I am five miles away. I also know that one centimeter on our map is equal to ten miles."

1. Using the ratio stated above, fill in the table to determine how far away the boat is from each station. For example, if a station's signal takes 16 seconds to reach the boat, set up the proportion:

$$\frac{2 \text{ seconds}}{5 \text{ miles}} = \frac{16 \text{ seconds}}{x \text{ miles}} \quad \begin{array}{l} (2 \times 8 = 16 \text{ seconds}) \\ (5 \times 8 = 40 \text{ miles}) \end{array} \quad 40 \text{ miles} = 4 \text{ centimeters on the map}$$

	Time it takes a signal to reach the boat	Distance from the boat to the station	Number of centimeters on the map
Station 1	20 seconds		
Station 2	18 seconds		
Station 3	32 seconds		

2. Use each distance recorded in the table as the radius of a circle. On your Sailing Circles Map, draw a circle from each station with the appropriate radius.

   When the three circles are drawn, there should be a triangle where the circles overlap. This triangle is called a "crooked hat." The boat is within the crooked hat.

3. What direction do Bryanna and Marquita have to travel to reach

   Corpus Christi? _____

4. About how far away are they from Corpus Christi? _____

5. Look at your Sailing Circles Map. Why are three circles needed to make the system work? Would two circles be enough? Write a brief

   explanation of your conclusion. _____

   _____

Hats Off to the Chef

30–45 minutes

OBJECTIVES

- Compute the area of circles, rectangles, and squares
- Make an organized list to determine various possibilities
- Make and justify a recommended solution

MATERIALS

- calculators
- Quarter-Inch Grid Paper, page 120 (optional)
- Math Notebook Page, page 119

TEACHER NOTES

This activity is intended to provide a real-world example of the use of area and problem-solving strategies. Listed below are suggested steps to follow for basic problem solving.

- Compute the area of the tray.

- Compute the area of each dessert.

- Determine how many of each dessert can be placed on a tray if only one type of dessert is used. Calculate the costs of these trays. A tray can hold 108 brownies at a cost of $54.00. A tray of 48 cupcakes costs $36.00. This provides some maximum numbers handy for the students.

- Begin listing possibilities of assortments. Include the number of each dessert, the total area, the arrangement on the tray, and the cost of the tray.

EXTENSIONS

- Determine a mark-up percentage and calculate the selling price for each tray. How much profit would be made?

- Determine the arrangement that would cost the least. (27 brownies + 36 cupcakes = $40.50)

- Create a spreadsheet to compute areas and costs of all combinations.

- Create a system of inequalities and a graph to determine feasible solutions.

ANSWERS

Answers will vary. To guide students through the process, lead a discussion and ask the following questions.

- How many square inches of space is the tray? (432 in.²)

- How many square inches of space will each brownie take? (4 in.²)

- How many square inches of space will each cupcake take? (9 in.². Each cupcake will take the area of a 3" × 3" square, not the area of a circle with a diameter of 3".)

- Since each arrangement needs to include at least a dozen of each dessert, how many total square inches of space will 12 brownies and 12 cupcakes take? (156 in.²)

- As you compute the areas for various arrangements, you will see that sometimes not every square inch of space is covered. Why is this true?

- Will more desserts fit on the tray if the desserts are arranged diagonally?

- Are there arrangements that cannot be made?

▶ Hats Off to the Chef

Chef Amy, a caterer, is designing a party tray of desserts. The tray is 18 inches wide and 24 inches long. The brownies are 2-inch squares. The cupcakes are 3 inches in diameter. Each dessert will be placed side by side in a single layer, to keep the icing fresh. Chef Amy wants to fill each tray completely. She must use at least a dozen of each dessert.

The manager, Rick, wants to know the different combinations of desserts that can be placed on the tray so that he can determine the cost of each tray. The cost for each brownie is $0.50 and each cupcake is $0.75.

Find the different combinations that could be created to fill a tray. Draw a picture of each design on your grid paper. You can draw other trays on the back of this page or on the back of the grid paper. Set up a chart, like the one shown, on your Math Notebook Page to help organize your data before you present your recommendation to manager Rick.

References to MATH ON CALL

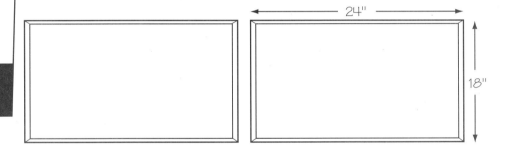

Tray	Brownies	Cupcakes	Cost
1			
2			
3			
4			

Which tray design would you recommend to manager Rick? _____

_____

Why? _____

_____

Geometry

High Guy

45–60 minutes

OBJECTIVES

- Use similar triangles to determine the height of a flagpole
- Apply trigonometric ratios to determine the height of a flagpole
- Determine the angle of elevation using an astrolabe

MATERIALS

- protractors
- yarn or string
- tape measures
- some item for weight such as 10 gram units, candy, a large nut, and so on

TEACHER NOTES

- This activity provides students with step-by-step directions to compute the height of tall objects. Flagpoles are a useful model.

- The Trig Method can be seen as a natural progression when students realize that shadows are not always manageable or available.

- Flagpoles are available in 3 styles. The most popular style is the tapered flag pole. For a 35' flag pole, the diameter at the base is 8" while the diameter at the top is 3". The other two styles are telescoping and non-tapered. The non-tapered pole is usually 15' or less in height. Determine what kind of flagpole you have.

EXTENSIONS

- When planting a flagpole, the hole must be four times as wide as the diameter of the flag pole. The hole must also be one foot deep for every 10 feet of pole. Given this information, what size hole was made to plant your school's flagpole?

- Use either method to determine the height of your school or any other building in your town.

ANSWERS

Shadow Reckoning

1. Students need to know the length of the flagpole's shadow, the length of a person's shadow, and the height of the same person.

2. The student can complete all the above measurements.

3. Measurements will vary. Check students' sketches.

4. $\dfrac{\text{student's height}}{\text{length of student's shadow}} = \dfrac{\text{flagpole height}}{\text{length of flagpole's shadow}}$

   The height of the flagpole will vary.

The Trig Method

5. Use the tangent ratio. The distance from the base of the pole to the student's standing position is the adjacent side of the triangle.

$$\text{Tangent of angle} = \frac{\text{height of flagpole}}{\text{distance from flagpole}}$$

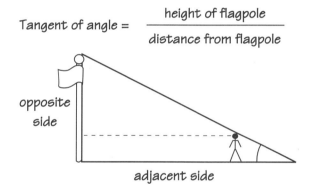

Be sure students add the distance from their eyes to the ground to the result of their calculations. The height of the flagpole should be close to the height obtained using the Shadow Reckoning method.

6. Using the Trig Method, the sun is not required to create a shadow. Since physical shadows are not necessary, the heights of buildings or mountains can be measured from many places.

▶ **High Guy**

Woodrow and Barney discovered that their dad had sat on top of a flagpole as a stunt. Woodrow wanted to determine the height of the pole. Help Barney and Woodrow research their dad's stunt.

Special Characteristics of Right Triangles: **358**

Similarity: **376**

Scale Drawings: **377**

Indirect Measurement: Proportions: **379**

Indirect Measurements: Trigonometric Ratios: **380**

References to MATH ON CALL

Shadow Reckoning

1. Refer to *Math on Call* item number 379. What pieces of information do you need to complete shadow reckoning for the height of the flagpole?

_____

2. Which measurements can be completed by a

student with a tape measure? _____

3. Measure the shadow of your school's flagpole and the length of the shadow of a student. Measure the height of the same student. On the back of this page, create a sketch of the pole, the student, the shadows, and the heights. Label the sketch with the measurements.

4. Set up the proportion and solve the proportion to determine the

height of the flagpole. _____

The Trig Method

To determine the angle of elevation, build an astrolabe. This can be done by tying a piece of string onto a protractor through the hole in the bottom center. Tie a weight at the other end of the string. Hold the protractor with the flat edge up and parallel to the ground, allowing the string to drop down. The string should cross the 90° mark on the protractor. Sight along the flat edge of the protractor and move it until it is in line with the top of the pole. Make a note of the measurement on the protractor for that angle. Subtract this measurement from 90° to determine the angle of elevation. Measure the distance from the base of the pole to where you are standing. Have a classmate measure the distance from your eyes to the ground.

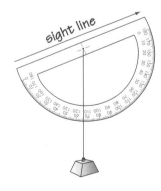

sight line

5. Determine which trigonometric ratio to use. Write that ratio and solve it. Add the distance from your eyes to the ground to your result

to find the height of the pole. _____

6. Why is the Trig Method a more favorable method than Shadow

Reckoning for determining height? _____

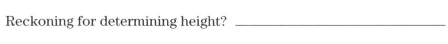

_____

Pass the Plate, Please

45–60 minutes

OBJECTIVES

• Relate fractions to degrees in circles
• Convert common fractions to degrees and show the correct proportion on a circle

MATERIALS

• foam or plastic plates with folds or ridges—each student will need two different-colored plates of the same size

TEACHER NOTES

• This activity requires the use of paper or foam plates that you will need to buy. Some plastic plates do not have the necessary folds or ridges around the circumference. Read through the student procedure to understand what is needed before you purchase the plates. The number of folds in a paper or foam plate should be the same if the plates are from the same manufacturer. Count the folds on the plates you buy to determine answers to some of the questions students are asked.

• Students need to start making connections between the folds on the plates and 360° in a circle. If there are 36 folds along the circumference of a plate, then there are 10° between each fold. If there are 72 folds on a plate, there are 5° between each fold, and so on.

• Once the plates have a cut to the center, have the students overlap them to make part of each color show on top. Determine which color will indicate the fraction. You may want to call out various fractions for them to estimate by rotating the plates. Have them make the fraction and then show you their plates. This is a quick check to see if they are relating the fractions to degrees in a circle.

• Have students actually convert sample fractions to degrees and determine how many folds would be necessary to make certain fractions.

EXTENSIONS

• Have students explore why manufacturers put folds on the plates. Suggest writing to a plate manufacturer to determine why the ridges are needed.

• Students can investigate different brands of plates at a local store. Compare the number of folds to the price. Is there any correlation? Compare also the size of the plate to the number of folds. Do different manufacturers put patterns on the rims of plates in a similar fashion? Do all paper plates with folds have a clear mathematical relationship with 360° in a circle? What about paper or foam bowls?

ANSWERS

1–3. Answers will vary depending on the number of folds on the plate.

4. 180°

5–6. Answers will vary. Check student drawings for good approximations of fractional parts of circles.

7. The fractions can be drawn because each denominator is a factor of 360.

▶ Pass the Plate, Please

**References to
MATH ON CALL**

Your teacher has given you two different-colored paper or foam plates of the same size. Notice the folds or ridges around the circumferences of the plates.

1. How many folds are there on one of the plates? _____

   Look up the references listed in the *Math on Call* Handbook.

2. What connections can you make between the information presented

   in *Math on Call* and the plates that you have? _____

   _____

3. How many degrees are there between the folds on the plate?

   _____

4. How many degrees of a circle are equal to the fraction $\frac{1}{2}$? _____

5. How many folds of your plate is that? _____

   Now cut a straight line into the center of each plate. Position the plates like the picture to the left. When you rotate one of the plates, you can demonstrate different fractional parts of the circle.

6. Rotate your plates to demonstrate each of the fractions listed below. Then draw each one on the circles provided.

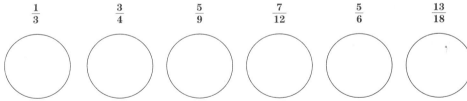

$\frac{1}{3}$ $\frac{3}{4}$ $\frac{5}{9}$ $\frac{7}{12}$ $\frac{5}{6}$ $\frac{13}{18}$

7. Why do you think it is possible to draw these fractional parts of a

   circle? _____

   _____

   _____

Don't Box Me In

30 minutes

OBJECTIVES

- Use patterns to understand square and cubic numbers
- Relate the area of a square to the exponent 2 and two-dimensional space
- Relate the volume of a cube to the exponent 3 and three-dimensional space

MATERIALS

- Quarter-Inch Grid Paper, page 120
- colored cubes (optional)

TEACHER NOTES

- This activity provides a link between the geometry of area and volume and the algebra of exponential notation. It features the common usage of the terms "squared" and "cubed" and connects those terms to the related geometric figures. Often students use the terms without any knowledge of the relationship to geometry.

- Connecting cubes can be used to create the larger cubes.

EXTENSIONS

- Determine which squares will nest within another square. When a square "nests," it should sit in the center and have an outline of complete squares. For example, a 1 by 1 square will nest inside a 3 by 3 square; a 2 by 2 square will nest inside a 4 by 4 square. Explore the relationship of the nesting squares with the students.

- Determine which cubes will nest within another cube. Explore this relationship with the students.

- Try this problem with the students. A cube with a side length of 5 units is painted on all sides, and then taken apart. How many of the smaller cubic units will have paint on 1 face only? Go on to discuss which ones will have paint on 2, 3, or no faces.

ANSWERS

1. 3
2. 4 square units
3. 5
4. 9 square units
5. The area is found the same way the number of squares is found, by multiplying the length by the width, or side by side, giving s^2 as the formula.
6. 2
7. x^2 can always represent the area of a square with side x.
8. 8
9. $3 \times 3 \times 3$
10. 27
11. 3
12. x^3 can always represent the volume of a cube with side x.
13. Area is two-dimensional and uses square measure while volume is three-dimensional and uses cubic measure.

▶ Don't Box Me In

**References to
MATH ON CALL**

On your grid paper, draw a square that is 1 unit on each side. Then add squares until you have a larger square that is 2 units on each side.

1. How many squares did you add? _____

2. What is the area of the new square? _____

   Now add squares to make a square that is 3 units on each side.

3. How many squares did you add? _____

4. What is the area of the new square? _____

5. How does the formula for the area of a square relate to the number of squares you used to create each larger square?

   _____

6. How many dimensions are used in finding the area of a square?

   _____

7. Why do you think the expression x^2 might be called "x squared?"

   _____

   Draw a cube that is one unit on each side. Add cubes until you have a larger cube that is 2 units on each side.

8. How many cubes are there in the larger cube? _____

   Now add cubes to make a cube that is 3 units on each side.

9. What are the dimensions of the new cube? _____

10. How many cubes are there in the larger cube? _____

11. How many dimensions are used in finding the area of a cube?

    _____

12. Why do you think the expression x^3 might be called "x cubed?"

    _____

13. In your own words, explain why area is measured in square units and volume is measured in cubic units.

    _____

    _____

A Monumental Net

45–60 minutes

OBJECTIVES

- Draw a net of a real-world building
- Calculate surface area of a real-world building

MATERIALS

- 1 cm Grid Paper, page 121, perhaps two sheets per student
- ruler or straightedge
- calculators

TEACHER NOTES

- The purpose of this activity is to help students visualize three-dimensional objects by creating two-dimensional nets. To create a net, students must mentally "view" an object or building from all sides and then identify the shape of each face.

- The word "sketch" is used intentionally to ease student apprehensions about drawing an exact scale model of the buildings.

EXTENSIONS

- Work with the students to calculate the volume of the inside hollow portion of the Washington Monument. You will need some additional measurements.

  - The side walls are 15 feet thick at the bottom and 18 inches thick at the top.

  - The sides of the pyramid are 7 inches thick.

- Have students do research to find the dimensions of the Lincoln Memorial in Washington, D.C. Then have them sketch the net and calculate the surface area of the building. The Jefferson Memorial provides an even greater challenge.

- Have students research the aluminum siding industry. They can investigate how the amount of necessary siding is determined for various applications.

- Collect various packages of grocery store items, such as cereal or detergent boxes. Have the students create the nets of these packages. How do the nets of the packages compare to nets of buildings?

- Students can investigate how architects plan and build scale models for presentation.

- Have students use scissors to cut out the nets and then build the shapes.

ANSWERS

1–2. Check student sketches for understanding of the shapes involved and some sense of the proportional relationship between them.

3. The Washington Monument in Washington, D.C.

4. Check student sketches as above.

5. Trapezoid

6. 2490.5 square yards. Student answers for this and the following calculations may vary depending on when and how often they round the results of their calculations.

7. Square

8. 337 square yards

9. Triangle

10. 110.5 square yards

11. 10,741 square yards

▶ A Monumental Net

Look at the sketch of a traditional house.

**References to
MATH ON CALL**

1. On your grid paper, sketch
the net of the house. Label the
following sections on your sketch:
front, rear, floor, right side, left side,
right gable, left gable, front roof,
and rear roof.

Here is some information about the dimensions of a famous building.

- The total height is 555 feet $5\frac{1}{8}$ inches.
- Each of its four sides is 55 feet $1\frac{1}{8}$ inches long at the bottom.
- The sides slant gradually inward toward the top and support a
  regular square pyramid with a height of 55 feet.
- Each side is 34 feet $5\frac{1}{2}$ inches long at the base of the pyramid.

2. Use this information to make a three-dimensional sketch of the
building on your grid paper. Your sketch doesn't need to be an exact
scale drawing, but should show an approximate proportional
relationship between the parts of the building.

3. What famous building is this? _____

4. Now sketch the net of this building on your grid paper.

For all calculations below, round the measurements to the nearest
inch. Express your answers in square yards.

5. What shape is each exposed face of the lower portion of the

building? _____

6. What is the surface area of each exposed face of the lower portion

of the building? _____

7. What shape is the floor space? _____

8. What is the surface area of the floor space? _____

9. What shape is each exposed face of the upper portion of the

building? _____

10. What is the surface area of each exposed face of the upper portion

of the building? _____

11. What is the surface area of the entire building? _____

Geometry

Souper Can

45–60 minutes

OBJECTIVES

- Calculate and compare the volume of cylinders
- Select a cylinder to use a given amount of shelf space to best advantage

MATERIALS

- calculators
- centimeter cubes, or other small objects that can be used to give an approximation of volume
- two sheets of 8.5" × 11" paper
- tape

TEACHER NOTES

- Students need to work in small groups for the first part of this activity, constructing and performing the experiment together. Then they make their predictions and answer the questions on their own.

EXTENSIONS

- Since the circumferences of the bases of the two cylinders used in the first part of the activity are known, have students prove mathematically that the volume of the cylinder with the larger radius has the greater volume.

- Have the students measure cans of various sizes and determine their volumes.

- Have students determine the net sales for a full shelf of each can of soup if the Regular can sells for $1.25 and the Special can sells for $1.35. Which shelf would yield the higher net sales?

- Introduce the concept of surface area and have students compare various cylinders to determine which can(s) have the best volume to surface area proportions. To calculate this, divide the surface area of each can by its volume. You can start with the two cans featured in this activity. Both cans have about the same volume, but the surface area of the Regular can is smaller, making it the more "efficient" of the two cans from the point of view of the cost of making the can. Think of an efficient can as one that holds the most within the smallest surface area. Mathematically, this will be cans with the smaller quotient when the surface area is divided by the volume.

- Research why manufacturers might choose to use a less efficient package. After arriving at a hypothesis, correspond with a manufacturer to determine if your hypothesis is correct.

ANSWERS

1. Check student predictions.

2. No, the 8.5" cylinder has the greater volume. Compare the results with student predictions.

3. The difference in volume is caused by the difference in the length of the radii of the two cans.

4.

Can	Radius	Diameter	Height	Volume
Regular can	1.5"	3"	4"	28.26 in.^{3}
Special can	2"	4"	2.25"	28.26 in.^{3}

5. More of the Regular can will fit on the shelf. It has a diameter of 3 inches, so there will be 16 cans in each layer, times 3 layers, or 48 cans. The Special can has a diameter of 4 inches, so each layer contains 9 cans, times 5 layers, or 45 cans.

6. Using the Regular can will put the most product on the shelf.

▶ Souper Can

DIRECTIONS

Circumference: 372

Pi: 373

Area of a Circle: 375

Cylinders: 409

Volume of Cylinders: 413

**References to
MATH ON CALL**

Take two sheets of 8.5" × 11" paper and curl one of them to form a cylinder 11" tall. Take the other sheet and curl it to form a cylinder 8.5" tall. Take a piece of tape and carefully join the edges of each cylinder. There should be no paper overlapping. Examine the two cylinders and predict if they will have the same or different volumes.

1. Check your prediction below.

    _____ The cylinders will have the same volume.

    _____ The cylinders will have different volumes, and the _____ inch-tall cylinder will have a greater volume.

Place the 11" cylinder upright on the table, so that the table forms the bottom of the cylinder. Fill the cylinder with centimeter cubes. While one person holds that cylinder, another person places the 8.5" cylinder over the 11" cylinder from the top. Both cylinders should be touching the table, and the 11" cylinder should be contained within the 8.5" cylinder. Now lift the 11" cylinder out slowly from the center.

2. Do the cylinders have the same volume? _____

3. Explain why or why not. _____

    _____

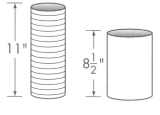

4. Your company is trying to determine the volume of two different-size cans of soup. Complete the following table.

Can	Radius	Diameter	Height	Volume
Regular can	1.5"		4"	
Special can	2"		2.25"	

5. The grocery store has given your company 12" of shelf space which is 12" deep and 12" high. How many cans of each style can you put on the shelf?

    _____ Regular cans   _____ Special cans

6. If price is not a factor, which can would you recommend using in

    order to put the most product on the shelf? _____

Toys R Real?

OBJECTIVES

- Use knowledge of proportions to determine if stuffed animals and their real counterparts have a proportional relationship
- Understand scale, ratio, and proportion

MATERIALS

- tape measure
- stuffed animals

45–60 minutes

TEACHER NOTES

- In this activity, students have the opportunity to revisit measurement, the concept of a fraction, and equivalent fractions, while investigating scale.

- You will need to ask students to bring a stuffed animal from home to school with them on the day you do this activity. You may need to supply some stuffed animals for those students who don't have one to bring to class.

- Before working with the stuffed animals, you may want to have students measure themselves and fill in a table similar to the one on their worksheet. Ask them to look for any patterns and proportional relationships that might show up. For example, is there a proportional relationship between the length of their hands and the length of their arms?

- Students will be comparing their stuffed animals to the corresponding real animal. Help them collect the dimensional information about real animals by supplying a telephone number for a nearby zoo, an Internet address such as www.sandiegozoo.org, or using the school or community library.

- Have students bring in other toys that have real counterparts, such as farm equipment, school buses, cars, dolls, and so on. Have them measure both the toy and the real thing and determine if there are any proportional relationships.

ANSWERS

1–4. Answers will vary. This activity encourages students to take measurements, record information, compare results, and draw conclusions. Check that they have an understanding of proportional relationships and know how to set up ratios to determine what those relationships are. Add your own observations of patterns and relationships to those the students have discovered.

EXTENSIONS

- Have students draw two-dimensional replicas for their animals and stuffed animals on grid paper. Determine the area of each. Compare body parts of the two drawings to determine if there is a relationship.

- Have students determine the ratio of arm length to total body length for both the stuffed and real animals. Are the ratios the same?

▶ **Toys R Real?**

**References to
MATH ON CALL**

You have brought a stuffed animal to class. Why? Because you are going to measure the dimensions of your stuffed animal, look for proportional relationships among those measurements, and then compare your stuffed animal to the real thing.

Complete the first column of the table below by measuring the described sections of your stuffed animal and recording the results in the table.

Look at the results you have recorded.

I. Do any of the measurements have a 2:1 ratio? _____

_____

2. If so, which measurements are they? _____

3. Write down any other patterns you see as you look at the

measurements. _____

_____

Obtain measurements for the real animal. To get these measurements, you may use resources in a library, call a zoo, or use the Internet. Complete the second column of the table with measurements from the real animal.

Compare the measurements of the stuffed animal to those of the real animal. Complete the third column of the table by computing the ratio between each section of your stuffed animal and the corresponding section of the real animal.

4. What conclusions can you make? Write a brief explanation to show whether or not the stuffed animal is proportional to the real animal.

_____

_____

	Stuffed animal	Real animal	Ratio
Length of body from top of head to bottom of feet			
Length of arm or wing			
Length of leg			
Length of body from top of shoulders to top of leg			
Circumference of head			
Circumference of neck			
Length of hand, paw, or claw			

Pedals and Sprockets and Gears, Oh My!

OBJECTIVES
• Compute gear ratios
• Determine distance traveled for different gear ratios

MATERIALS
• calculators

30–45 minutes

TEACHER NOTES

• Bicycles are an important mode of transportation for middle-school students. This activity is intended to spark interest in the mechanics of the bicycle. Most students will not be familiar with the terminology used. For example, in most cases the words *sprockets* and *teeth* have the same meaning. When referring to bicycles, however, the word *sprockets* is used to mean the gears around which the bicycle chain passes.

• Cyclists try to maintain the same pedaling speed. The highest gear is defined to have the greatest gear ratio. This is the largest sprocket on the chainwheel, and the smallest sprocket on the freewheel. Gears are chosen to maintain a consistent pedaling speed, low gears for going up slopes, high gears for going down slopes.

• Information for this activity is from *The Tour De France, Complete Book of Cycling*, David Chauner and Michael Halstead, Villard Books, New York, 1990.

ANSWERS

Tour de Cycle			Really Racing		
Gear Name	Gear Ratio	Roll-Out (in feet)	Gear Name	Gear Ratio	Roll-Out (in feet)
39–14	72	19	30–14	56	15
39–17	60	16	30–17	46	12
39–20	51	13	30–21	37	10
39–24	42	11	30–24	33	9
39–29	35	9	30–29	27	7
50–14	93	24	39–14	72	19
50–17	76	20	39–17	60	16
50–20	65	17	39–21	48	13
50–24	54	14	39–24	42	11
50–29	45	12	39–29	35	9
			50–14	93	24
			50–17	76	20
			50–21	62	16
			50–24	54	14
			50–29	45	12

EXTENSIONS

• Have students determine the gear ratios of their own bikes.

• Using the data from the completed table, students can calculate how many pedal revolutions it will take to travel one mile using different gear ratios.

• Students can time someone cycling a set distance to determine the rate in miles per hour. They can experiment by changing gear ratios to see how the rate changes.

1. As the gear ratio increases, the roll-out also increases.

2. A gear ratio of 93 allows a cyclist to travel 24 feet for each revolution of the pedals.

▶ Pedals and Sprockets and Gears, Oh My!

Range: 272

Pi: 373

Ratio: 424

Multiple-Step
  Conversions: 437

Counting Principle: 459

Make a Table or an
  Organized List: 480

**References to
MATH ON CALL**

Matt wanted to buy a mountain bike. He was comparing the Tour de Cycle and Really Racing bikes. The main difference between the two bikes was that the number of sprockets and teeth on the pedal (chainwheel) and back wheel (freewheel) were not the same. Matt did some research and discovered that the number of sprockets and the number of teeth on each sprocket, determine the range of gear ratios for a bike. Gear names are determined by the ratio of the chainwheel teeth to the freewheel teeth.

Tour de Cycle 26" Wheel					
Wheel	Number of Teeth				
Chainwheel	39	50			
Freewheel	14	17	20	24	29

Really Racing 26" Wheel					
Wheel	Number of Teeth				
Chainwheel	30	39	50		
Freewheel	14	17	21	24	29

Use the information in the two tables above to create a list of all possible gear names for each bike. Enter the gear names in the table below.

The gear ratio is calculated by using the formula:

$$\text{gear ratio} = \frac{\text{number of chainwheel teeth}}{\text{number of freewheel teeth}} \times \text{size of wheel}$$

Determine the gear ratios for each brand of bike. Round your calculations to the nearest whole number. Enter the ratios in the table.

Tour de Cycle			Really Racing		
Gear Name	Gear Ratio	Roll-Out (in feet)	Gear Name	Gear Ratio	Roll-Out (in feet)
39–14	72	19	30–14	56	
39–17					
			30–24		
50–24					
50–29					
			50–17		

The roll-out of a gear is the distance traveled with one complete revolution of the pedals. The roll-out, in inches, is calculated by multiplying the gear ratio by π. Determine the roll-out, in feet, of each gear for each brand of bike. Round your calculations to the nearest whole number and enter them in the table.

1. What relationship do you see between the gear ratio and the roll-out of the gears?

_____

_____

2. Which gear ratio from the table allows a cyclist to travel the greatest distance with one revolution of the pedals?

_____

▶ Boxing for Gold

OBJECTIVE

- Approximate the Golden Ratio using the Fibonacci Sequence

MATERIALS

- calculators
- Quarter-Inch Grid Paper, page 120
- colored pencils

30–45 minutes

TEACHER NOTES

- The Golden Ratio is also called the Golden Proportion or the Golden Section. It occurs widely in art, architecture, music, package design, and nature. You may want to have students measure to find the ratio of their height to the length from their waist to the floor, which also approximates the Golden Ratio. The same is true of the ratio of the length of their faces to the width of their faces.

- This activity also demonstrates the swirling nature of the Fibonacci Sequence through the repetitive sketches of rectangles.

- The exact value of the golden ratio is $1 + \frac{\sqrt{5}}{2}$. The decimal approximation is 1.618.

EXTENSIONS

- Point out to the students that in the world around us there are many Golden Rectangles. Students can examine index cards, photographs, books, and boxes to see how the sides relate to each other. Other examples might include paintings, windows in a house, or in-ground swimming pools.

- Have students create a Golden Rectangle on tracing paper. Then lay the tracing paper over pictures of paintings, buildings, or windows to see applications of the Golden Ratio.

- Have students draw a regular pentagon and its diagonals. Measure the lengths of the segments of the diagonals. Find the pairs of segments that display the Golden Ratio.

- Design a spreadsheet to help you generate the numbers in the Fibonacci Sequence.

ANSWERS

Fibonacci number	New Fibonacci number	Ratio
0		
1	1	1
1	2	2
2	3	1.5
3	5	1.667
5	8	1.6
8	13	1.625
12	21	1.615
21	34	1.619
34	55	1.618
55	89	1.618
89	144	1.618

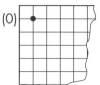
▶ Boxing for Gold

Fibonacci Sequence: **546**

Golden Ratio: **547**

**References to
MATH ON CALL**

The Fibonacci Sequence and the Golden Ratio have long been known to
have an intriguing relationship. Using grid paper and a calculator, you
are about to find a close approximation for the Golden Ratio.

Directions

- Make a dot at the intersection of two lines at the
  upper left corner of your grid paper. This dot represents 0, the first term of the Fibonacci Sequence.

- From this point draw a square that is 1 unit by 1 unit. These two
  dimensions are the second and third terms of the Fibonacci Sequence.

1. Write the decimal value of 1 ÷ 1. _____

Using a different-colored pencil, add a second
square to the right of the first one so that the
resulting rectangle is 2 units by 1 unit. Two is the
fourth term in the Fibonacci Sequence.

2. Write the decimal value of 2 ÷ 1. _____

Use a different-colored pencil. To the longer side of
your rectangle, add a square with a side length of 2
units (the length of the longer side of the rectangle).
Your new rectangle is 3 units by 2 units. The longer
dimension (3) is the next term in the Fibonacci Sequence.

3. Write the decimal value of 3 ÷ 2. _____

Using a different-colored pencil, add a square to the
longer side of this rectangle.

4. Find the decimal value of $\dfrac{\text{length (longer side)}}{\text{width (shorter side)}}$.

Repeat the pattern of adding a square to the longer side of each
rectangle until you have filled your grid paper. Draw each rectangle
with a new color and determine the decimal value of the ratio
between the length of the longer and the length of the shorter sides.

5. Complete the table on the left. Remember that each new Fibonacci
number is the sum of the two preceding Fibonacci numbers. The first
entries summarize what you have already completed. Round each
decimal value to the nearest thousandth.

Notice that as the numbers grow larger, the decimal value of the ratio
approaches and then remains at 1.618 when rounded to the nearest
thousandth. If you had space on your grid paper to draw rectangles
this large, you would be looking at closer and closer representations
of Golden Rectangles. These are rectangles whose sides relate to each
other in the Golden Ratio.

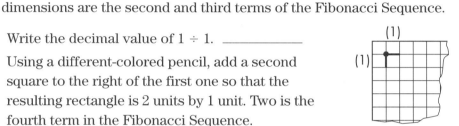

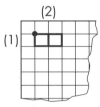

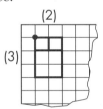

Fibonacci number	New Fibonacci number	Ratio
0		
1	1	1
1	2	2
2	3	1.5
3	5	
5		

It Costs How Much?

45–60 minutes

OBJECTIVES

- Compare differing rates by calculating the unit rate
- Develop three plans to spend a budgeted amount of money

MATERIALS

- calculators

TEACHER NOTES

- In a major newspaper, the number of columns varies depending on the section. For example, the classified section has many more columns than the front page. For purposes of this activity, the prices are based on 6 two-inch columns across the page which is 21 inches long.

- Question 4 asks students to decide how to spend $10,000 three different ways. Most students have a hard time deciding how to spend $20. Thinking about how to spend a large amount of money over time is challenging. The question attempts to get students to recognize that planning is a part of life.

EXTENSIONS

- Have students research the cost of advertising in other media, such as radio, television, and the Internet. Calculate a per person cost for these other media and compare.

- Research shows that the more frequently a store name is seen or heard, the more likely a person is to shop there. With this in mind, what is the maximum number of times an ad can be placed in the newspaper in one month with only $10,000 to spend?

- An ad that is too small will not be noticed. See if students can determine which size ad is most effective. They should contact both the newspaper publisher and businesses that buy advertising space to arrive at a fair conclusion.

ANSWERS

1.

Space	Daily rate*	Cost per subscriber	Sunday rate**	Cost per subscriber
1" of 1 column	$57.75	$0.00057	$66.50	$0.00056
quarter-page	$1819.00	$0.01808	$2095.00	$0.01775
half-page	$3639.50	$0.03618	$4190.50	$0.03551
full-page	$7276.50	$0.07234	$8379.00	$0.07101

* daily circulation = 100,583

** Sunday circulation = 117,996

2. The number of people who see the advertisement is 58,998. $8379 ÷ 58,998 = $0.14202

3. $1819 ÷ 118,325 = $0.01537

4. Answers will vary. Check student work for understanding of the concepts needed to spend a budgeted amount of money in an effective way.

▶ It Costs How Much?

**References to
MATH ON CALL**

The advertising manager for Robot-techs, an electronics store, is planning his proposal for newspaper ads for the month of October. The table below shows the costs of different-size ads in the local newspaper. Different amounts are charged for ads that appear in the Sunday edition.

Space	Daily rate*	Cost per subscriber	Sunday rate**	Cost per subscriber
1" of 1 column	$57.75		$66.50	
quarter-page	$1819.00		$2095.00	
half-page	$3639.50		$4190.50	
full-page	$7276.50		$8379.00	

* daily circulation = 100,583

** Sunday circulation = 117,996

1. Calculate the cost per subscriber for each type of advertisement shown in the table.

2. How much per subscriber would a full-page advertisement cost on a Sunday if only half the circulation sees the advertisement?

   _____

3. The daily circulation just went up to 118,325. What is the cost per subscriber for a quarter-page advertisement now?

   _____

4. Robot-techs has budgeted $10,000 for newspaper ads during the month of October. Develop three proposals for spending this money. Each proposal must include more than one advertisement. In order to get more money for advertising in the future, the advertising manager needs to spend as much of the money as he can without going over budget.

Momma, Can I Have . . .?

30-45 minutes

OBJECTIVES

• Compute and compare unit prices
• Make an arrangement of products based on unit prices

MATERIALS

• calculators
• Math Notebook Page, page 119

TEACHER NOTES

• The grocery store provides multiple opportunities for students to use decimals and rates. Understanding unit pricing is critical when shopping for determining the best buy.

• Students should be aware that stores may not always advertise or prominently display the most economical product.

• Students should also realize that brand-name products are given greater shelf space and higher prices than the store brand.

EXTENSIONS

• Have students make a map of an aisle at a local grocery store. They can also map the same products at two or more stores and compare arrangements and unit prices.

• Call the marketing manager for a grocery store chain and investigate how display plans are developed.

• Map the entire grocery store and compare the products and unit prices to the placement of the items.

ANSWERS

1. The top 2 shelves

2. The bottom 2 shelves

3. The top 3 shelves

4. The bottom 3 shelves

5.

Cereal	Size	Cost	Unit price (cents)	Cookies	Size	Cost	Unit price (cents)
Frosted Grains*	12.5 oz	$3.29	26.32¢	Fig Bars	18 oz	$1.99	11.06¢
Chocolate Rice	20.25 oz	$3.79	18.72¢	Sugar Cookies	16 oz	$3.29	20.56¢
Crispy Oats*	11.25 oz	$3.09	27.47¢	Ginger Wafers	17 oz	$3.29	19.35¢
Frosted Oats	14 oz	$3.19	22.79¢	Vanilla Snaps	10.5 oz	$2.79	26.57¢
Crispy Rice	20 oz	$3.99	19.95¢	Chocolate Sandwich	14 oz	$2.89	20.64¢
Frosted Wheat*	10 oz	$2.59	25.90¢	Cream Wafers	16 oz	$1.99	12.44¢
Circle-O Oats*	15 oz	$3.19	21.27¢	Fudge Bars	11 oz	$3.19	29.00¢
Sports Flakes*	13.7 oz	$3.29	24.01¢	Pecan Nutters	11.5 oz	$2.19	19.04¢
Jumbo Oats	35 oz	$6.23	17.80¢	Chocolate Chip	13.5 oz	$2.99	22.15¢

* Cereals with special promotional items for children

6. Maps will vary. Check student work to see if they recognize that items with high unit prices that are easily visible to adults should be placed on the upper shelves. Items with high unit prices and special appeal for children should be placed on the lower shelves. Items with the lowest unit prices should be placed on the lowest shelf.

▶ Momma, Can I Have . . .?

Dividing with Decimals:
   184

Rate: 435

Unit Price: 438

Comparing Unit Prices to
   Find the Better
   Buy: 439

**References to
MATH ON CALL**

Research shows that most consumers buy products displayed at eye level in the grocery store. The manager of the local grocery store assigns you the job of rearranging the cereal and cookie sections to test the research. The cereal section has 4 shelves that are 18 inches apart. The cookie section has 6 shelves that are 12 inches apart. The bottom shelf is always about one foot above floor level.

1. Which cereal shelves would be nearest eye level for the average adult shopper? _____

2. Which cookie shelves would be nearest eye level for the average adult shopper? _____

3. Which cereal shelves would be nearest eye level for the average 6-year-old child? _____

4. Which cookie shelves would be nearest eye level for the average 6-year-old child? _____

5. The table shows the cereal and cookie products with the size and price of each package. Determine the unit price for each item. Round to the nearest hundredth of a cent.

Cereal	Size	Cost	Unit price (cents)	Cookies	Size	Cost	Unit price (cents)
Frosted Grains*	12.5 oz	$3.29		Fig Bars	18 oz	$1.99	
Chocolate Rice	20.25 oz	$3.79		Sugar Cookies	16 oz	$3.29	
Crispy Oats*	11.25 oz	$3.09		Ginger Wafers	17 oz	$3.29	
Frosted Oats	14 oz	$3.19		Vanilla Snaps	10.5 oz	$2.79	
Crispy Rice	20 oz	$3.99		Chocolate Sandwich	14 oz	$2.89	
Frosted Wheat*	10 oz	$2.59		Cream Wafers	16 oz	$1.99	
Circle-O Oats*	15 oz	$3.19		Fudge Bars	11 oz	$3.19	
Sports Flakes*	13.7 oz	$3.29		Pecan Nutters	11.5 oz	$2.19	
Jumbo Oats	35 oz	$6.23		Chocolate Chip	13.5 oz	$2.99	

* Cereals with special promotional items for children

6. On the back of this page, draw a map of the cereal and cookie sections. Show where you would place each product. Remember that you want to sell items with high unit prices. Then write an explanation of the reasoning behind your arrangement on your Math Notebook Page.

Getting a Census of Growth

OBJECTIVES

- Analyze information in a table
- Understand how percent shows change
- Understand how to calculate percent of change over time

MATERIALS

- a copy of the Census Data table on page 125 for each student
- calculators (optional)

30–45 minutes

TEACHER NOTES

- This is a good activity to use with other content areas, such as history, economics, or geography. Encourage students to connect other topics they are studying with the numbers in the table. This can help them make good guesses about why population can change so dramatically over time.

EXTENSIONS

- Have students research the history and economy of a particular city and hypothesize why the population may have changed the way it did.

- Compare regional populations and their changes with the students. Does a general decrease in population for northern cities result in a corresponding increase in population for southern cities? What about eastern and western cities?

- Ask students to hypothesize about why the populations of some cities, such as Cincinnati or Philadelphia, remain relatively constant over time.

- See if students can identify significant historical events in United States or world history that may have played a role in the population changes over a 10- or 20-year period. Other cities can also be included.

- Suggest that the students compare population changes in a major city with changes in the population of nearby suburbs and rural communities.

ANSWERS

1. Seattle had a 76.7% increase in population between 1920 and 1960.

2. New York City had a 10% decrease in population between 1950 and 1980.

3. Houston shows the largest percent of increase in population from 1920 to 1990. The percent of increase was 1079%. This means that the population of Houston was about 10 times larger in 1990 than in 1920.

4. Jacksonville experienced a 163% increase in population between 1960 and 1970.

5. With a 17.5% increase in population, Los Angeles has grown the fastest since 1980. Jacksonville is not far behind with a 17.4% increase.

▶ Getting a Census of Growth

**References to
MATH ON CALL**

Take a look at the Census Data table your teacher has given to you. As you look at the changes in city populations over time, begin to think about some factors that might contribute to those changes. Immigration is one thing that can affect population growth. Consider major immigration points such as New York, Los Angeles, or Houston. Immigration probably accounts for some of the rapid population growth of these cities when compared to the population growth of inland cities such as Cincinnati, Denver, or Atlanta. As you look at the Census Data table, use what you know about historical events and population trends to make educated guesses about why city populations change in relation to time, geography, and history.

Use the chart to answer these questions.

1. What percent of increase in population did Seattle have from 1920 to 1960?

   _____

   _____

2. What percent of decrease in population did New York City have from 1950 to 1980?

   _____

   _____

3. Which city had the largest percent of increase in population from 1920 to 1990? What was the percent of increase?

   _____

   _____

4. The 1970 Census was the first time cities could include the population of incorporated rural areas in the city population count. This explains the dramatic increase for Jacksonville, Florida. What percent of increase in population did Jacksonville have from 1960 to 1970?

   _____

   _____

5. Which city has had the largest percent of increase in population since 1980? Which city has grown almost as fast since 1980?

   _____

   _____

An Incredit-Card-Able Purchase

45–60 minutes

OBJECTIVES

- Compute compound interest
- Compare total costs

MATERIALS

- Incredit-Card Page, page 122
- calculators

TEACHER NOTES

- This activity gives students an opportunity to compare the interest paid using a credit card to the interest lost from a savings account when cash is used for a purchase.

- Have students use the compound interest formula found in *Math on Call* to determine the amount of interest paid for the savings account, both with and without the stereo purchase.

- Make sure students understand that paying off the credit card, when the balance after payment falls below $100.00, significantly shortens the life of the loan. If the minimum payment is made consistently, it would take more than five years to pay off the credit card.

EXTENSIONS

- Have students investigate annual percentage rates for car loans when purchasing a new or used car.

- Students can investigate the amount of interest actually paid when a company advertises no interest for 6 months, and then begins charging interest.

- Have students determine a standard monthly payment amount on the credit card stereo purchase so that the stereo is completely paid for in one year and the interest paid is less than the interest lost on the savings account.

ANSWERS

1. $1277.96
2. $5215.91
3. $3722.04
4. $3882.77
5. $55.18
6. $102.68
7. $149.62
8. $1427.58
9. 32 months
10. Answers will vary. Students should be able to justify their conclusions.

An Incredit-Card-Able Purchase

**References to
MATH ON CALL**

You have just gotten your first part-time job and plan to purchase a new stereo system on sale. The stereo is marked 20% off the regular price of $1499.95. The sales tax is 6.5%.

Use this information to compare the relative costs of your relatives' information.

Uncle Joe

Uncle Joe, the financial wizard, says, "Establish your credit!"

Cousin Carol

Cousin Carol says, "Use your savings!"

Credit Card
Monthly Interest 1.02%
Minimum Payment 9% of Balance

Savings Account
Balance $5000
Anual Percentage Rate 4.25%
Paid Quarterly

1. What is the cost of the stereo including tax? _____
   Calculate your cost using Cousin Carol's method.
   Current balance: $5000.00

2. Savings account balance after 1 year without purchase: _____

3. Principal after purchase: _____

4. Savings account balance after 1 year with purchase: _____

5. Interest lost by withdrawing money: _____

   Now calculate your cost using Uncle Joe's credit card plan. Using a calculator, complete the table on your Incredit-Card Page. Pay only the 9% Minimum Payment each month. Round the calculations to the nearest cent after each step. When the balance after payment is below $100.00, you can pay it off.

6. How much interest will you pay over the course of the first year?

   _____

7. How much interest will you pay over the life of the loan? _____

8. How much will you pay for the stereo all together using the credit
   card? _____

9. How many months will it take to pay off the credit card? _____

10. Based on your calculations, write an explanation of which plan you
    would choose and why.

    _____

    _____

Probability and Odds

Number, Please

45–60 minutes

OBJECTIVES

• Determine theoretical probability
• Calculate experimental probability

MATERIALS

• a page from an old telephone book for each student

TEACHER NOTES

• Students will first calculate the theoretical probability of the last digit of a telephone number.

• The telephone book used should be an old one. It is really convenient to tear a page out of the telephone book, count off 100 numbers, and start to tally.

• A telephone number consists of 10 digits. Usually, for a local call only the last 7 digits are needed. However, in large cities, all 10 digits must be used due to the large number of fax machines, pagers, and cellular telephones. For this activity, look at the last of the 10 digits to collect the data.

EXTENSIONS

• With the onset of 10-digit phone numbers, has the experimental probability grown closer or farther from the theoretical probability?

• Originally, the middle digit of an area code had to be 0 or 1. Knowing that the first digit of the area code cannot be 0 or 1, how many combinations were there for area codes?

• Research the history of telephone numbers and determine if there were any other patterns in the numbers.

ANSWERS

1. The theoretical probability of a 4 in the last position is 1 out of 10. This is calculated by determining all the possible outcomes (0, 1, 2, 3, 4, 5, 6, 7, 8, 9) and determining the ratio of the selected outcome to the total possible outcomes. (If only business telephone numbers are used, 0 may occur more often. If only residential telephone numbers are used, 0 may occur less often.)

2. Answers will vary.

3. The larger the sample space, the closer the probability will get to 10%.

4. The tallies would definitely look different if the first position is used. The numbers 0 and 1 cannot be used in the first position because they are generic numbers reserved for assistance and long-distance calls. Usually, in a given city or town, there are only one or two digits that are used for the first digit.

▶ Number, Please

Shannon knew that any of the digits 0 through 9 could occur as the last digit of a telephone number. She wondered if any of the digits occur more often than the others.

How Likely Is an
   Event?: 462

Sample Space: 463

Probability of an Event: 465

Theoretical and
   Experimental
   Probability: 466

**References to
MATH ON CALL**

1. What is the theoretical probability of a four in the last position of a

   telephone number? _____

2. Count off 100 telephone numbers on a page from the telephone book. Place a tally mark next to the number below for each time it appears as the last digit of a telephone number. After making the tallies, calculate the fraction, decimal, and percent equivalencies for each digit.

	Tally	Fraction	Decimal	Percent
0				
1				
2				
3				
4				
5				
6				
7				
8				
9				

3. Total your tallies with 9 other members of your class. Recalculate the fraction, decimal, and percent equivalencies. Are your new results

   closer to the theoretical probability? _____

   _____

4. Would the results be very different if the number in the first position

   of a 7-digit telephone number was used? Why or why not? _____

   _____

112

Target Practice

OBJECTIVE

• Determine the ratio of a favorable area to a total area

MATERIALS

• calculators

30–45 minutes

TEACHER NOTES

• Geometric probability is an extension usually reserved for advanced geometry courses yet is easily understood by a middle-school student.

• This activity encourages students to use area formulas within the context of probability.

EXTENSIONS

• Have students design a target and play a game with points awarded based on the probability for each area.

• Analyze other target games, such as throwing darts at a balloon, or rings on a bottle, to try to determine the probabilities of success.

• Research archery to determine how scoring is computed.

• Research which Olympic sports include a point system for targets.

ANSWERS

1. 100 m^2

2. 64 m^2

3. $\frac{64}{100}$ or 0.64

4. $25\pi - 16\pi = 9\pi \text{ in.}^2$

5. $16\pi - 9\pi = 7\pi \text{ in.}^2$

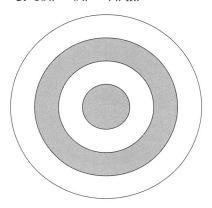

6. $9\pi - 4\pi = 5\pi \text{ in.}^2$

7. $4\pi \text{ in.}^2$

8. $25\pi \text{ in.}^2$

9. $\frac{9}{25}$ or 0.36

10. $\frac{7}{25}$ or 0.28

11. $\frac{5}{25}$ or 0.2

12. $\frac{4}{25}$ or 0.16

13. $\frac{14}{25}$ or 0.56

14. $\frac{11}{25}$ or 0.44

▶ Target Practice

Geometric probability is the ratio of the favorable area to the possible area.

Suppose you plan to hit a target like the one shown. The inside square is the favorable area of the target.

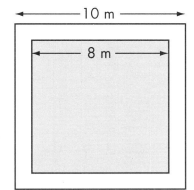

1. First, find the area of the

   whole square. _____

2. Then find the area of the

   inside square. _____
   The ratio of the $\dfrac{\text{favorable area}}{\text{area of the whole square}}$
   is the probability you can hit the shaded area.

3. What is that probability? _____

**References to
MATH ON CALL**

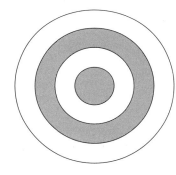

Suppose you plan to hit this circular dart board. The outer circle diameter is 10 inches, the second diameter is 8 inches, the inner diameter is 6 inches, and the bull's-eye diameter is 4 inches.

For questions 4–8, express your answers in terms of π.

4. What is the area of the outer ring? _____

5. What is the area of the second ring? _____

6. What is the area of the inner ring? _____

7. What is the area of the bull's-eye? _____

8. What is the area of the whole dart board? _____

Use your answers from questions 4–8 to solve these questions.

9. What is the probability of hitting the outer ring? _____

10. What is the probability of hitting the second ring? _____

11. What is the probability of hitting the inner ring? _____

12. What is the probability of hitting the bull's-eye? _____

13. What is the probability of hitting a white area? _____

14. What is the probability of hitting a shaded area? _____

Is That Fair?

OBJECTIVES

- Compute the probability of events
- Compute the expected value for a player
- Decide whether a game is fair

MATERIALS

30–45 minutes

TEACHER NOTES

- Some games favor one player over another. To decide whether a game is fair, compute the expected value for each player. The expected value of a player is determined by multiplying the probability of winning by the amount won.

- The probability of an event occurring is the ratio of the number of favorable outcomes to the number of possible outcomes.

EXTENSIONS

- Students can evaluate existing games to determine their fairness.

- Students can design their own games and decide whether the games are fair.

ANSWERS

1. Answers will vary.

2. Player with green:

   Expected value $= \left(\frac{1}{8} \times 7\right) + \left(\frac{1}{8} \times 2\right) = \frac{9}{8}$

   Player with yellow:

   Expected value $= \left(\frac{1}{8} \times 3\right) + \left(\frac{1}{8} \times 6\right) = \frac{9}{8}$

   Player with blue:

   Expected value $= \left(\frac{1}{8} \times 4\right) + \left(\frac{1}{8} \times 5\right) = \frac{9}{8}$

3. Yes, the game is fair because each player's expected value is the same.

4. There are eight possible outcomes: HHH, HHT, HTH, THH, TTH, THT, HTT, TTT

5. Answers will vary. One possibility is:

   Player A gets 12 points. $\frac{1}{8} \times 12 = \frac{12}{8} = \frac{3}{2}$

   Player B gets 4 points. $\frac{3}{8} \times 4 = \frac{12}{8} = \frac{3}{2}$

   Player C gets 3 points. $\frac{4}{8} \times 3 = \frac{12}{8} = \frac{3}{2}$

Probability and Odds

▶ **Is That Fair?**

Multiplying a Whole
  Number by a
  Fraction: 161

Probability of an
  Event: 465

Theoretical and
  Experimental
  Probabiltiy: 466

Odds: 471–472

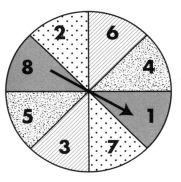

**References to
MATH ON CALL**

You and three friends are playing a game. Each player picks a color on the spinner and takes a turn spinning the spinner. When the spinner stops on a color, the player with that color receives the number of points shown on the spinner. The first person with 100 points wins the game. Is this a fair game?

A game is fair if each player has an equal chance of winning. This means that if you play a game many times, each player can expect to win about the same number of times. If the game is fair, the expected value of a spin must be the same for each player. The expected value of a spin for a player is the probability of landing on a player's color times the number of points won. For example, the expected value for the player with red is:

$$\text{Expected value} = \left(\frac{1}{8} \times 1\right) + \left(\frac{1}{8} \times 8\right) = \frac{1}{8} + \frac{8}{8} = \frac{9}{8}.$$

1. Without calculating the expected value for each player, do you think this is a fair game? Explain your answer.

_____

_____

2. Determine the expected value for the remaining three players.

_____

_____

3. Is this a fair game? Explain your answer.

_____

_____

4. You and two friends are playing another game. Each player tosses a coin. How many possible outcomes are there for how the coins will land? What are the possible outcomes?

_____

_____

5. You and your two friends decide that if there are exactly three heads, player A will get the points. If there are exactly two heads, player B will get the points. If there are exactly one or zero heads, player C will get the points. How many points should each player get to make this a fair game? Explain your answer.

_____

_____

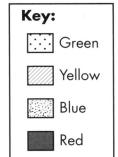

Key:

▫ Green

▨ Yellow

▨ Blue

■ Red

Probability and Odds

▶ One If by Land . . .

OBJECTIVES

• Determine the total number of possible permutations
• Make organized lists
• Draw diagrams to solve problems

MATERIALS

• Math Notebook Page, page 119
• colored cubes or construction paper (optional)

30–45 minutes

TEACHER NOTES

• Communication with friends is a high priority for young adolescents. This activity ties mathematics to communication, also a real-world necessity.

• Students may need to build models to create the possibilities. Colored cubes are a useful manipulative. The students will need to assign the colors of the lights to the available colors of cubes. Construction paper cut in small squares will also work.

• The possibilities for the first question can be modeled. The second list gets rather lengthy and necessitates the use of an organized plan rather than building all the models.

EXTENSIONS

• Try adding another row of window panes or a flashlight in a fourth color with the students. This expands the possibilities and will demand the use of an organized list.

• Many graphing calculators include programs that will compute permutations and combinations. If you have access to such a calculator, show students how it works and create new scenarios for them to solve using the calculator.

• Students may want to investigate Morse code, flags, and other communication systems.

ANSWERS

1. There are 9 possibilities. Since order is important, then $_3P_2 = 3 \times 2 = 6$ permutations using two flashlights. With one flashlight, $_3P_1 = 3 \times 1 = 3$ possible permutations.

RY	*YR*	*R*
RW	*WR*	*Y*
YW	*WY*	*W*

2. A total of 93 signals can be created. There are 3 different color pairs: *RY*, *RW*, and *WY*. First find the number of different signals for one pair. If *R* is in the first pane, these signals can be made with *R* and *Y*:

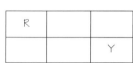

So there are 5 possibilities. Multiply 5 by 6 since *R* can be in any of the 6 panes. That will give *all* the possibilities for *R* and *Y*. (30)

Since there are 3 different color pairs, multiply 30 by 3 to get the total number of possibilities for two-color pairs. Add the 3 possibilities for one-color signals. (90 + 3 = 93)

▶ One If by Land . . .

Best friends Lee and Pat found three different flashlights. One glowed red, one glowed yellow, and the third one glowed white. They discovered that with these flashlights they could send signals to each other from window to window across their street. Soon they realized only two flashlights could be held at one time. The windows are pictured below.

1. Using three colors and two hands, how many different signals could be sent? List the possibilities.

_____

_____

_____

Next our clever friends decided that more signals could be created if they could use the different window panes to determine the position of the lights. By experimentation they discovered that space between the colors could be distinguished, like those pictured, and lights could be seen. However, when only one light was used, the position of the light in the pane could not be determined.

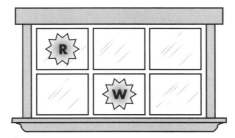

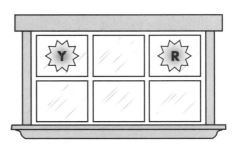

2. Determine how many different signals can be created. Use models to get started. Record your method for finding the total on your Math Notebook Page.

Numeric Pagers	Cool Communiqués		Fetch-A-Friend	
	Function: $\$13.00m$	Total cost	Function: $\$39.00 + \$15.00 + \$8.95m$	Total cost
1 month				
3 months				
6 months				
9 months				
12 months				
15 months				
n months				

Alpha-Numeric Pagers	Cool Communiqués		Fetch-A-Friend	
	Function:	Total cost	Function:	Total cost
1 month				
3 months				
6 months				
9 months				
12 months				
15 months				
n months				

My Math Notebook

▶ **Topic** _____

Examples

Quarter-Inch Grid Paper   Name _____

Month	Balance	1.02% Interest	New balance	Minimum payment (9% of new balance)	Balance after payment
1	$1277.96	$13.04	$1291.00	$116.19	$1174.81
2	$1174.81				
3					
4					
5					
6					
7					
8					
9					
10					
11					
12					
13					
14					
15					
16					
17					
18					
19					
20					
21					
22					
23					
24					
25					
26					
27					
28					
29					
30					
31					
32					
33					
34					
35					

Look Out Below! Game Board

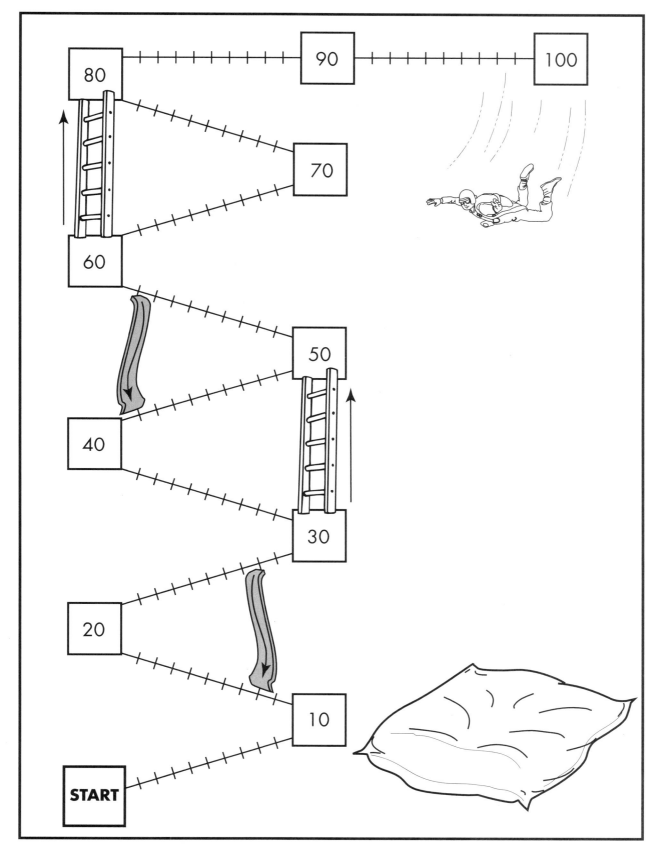

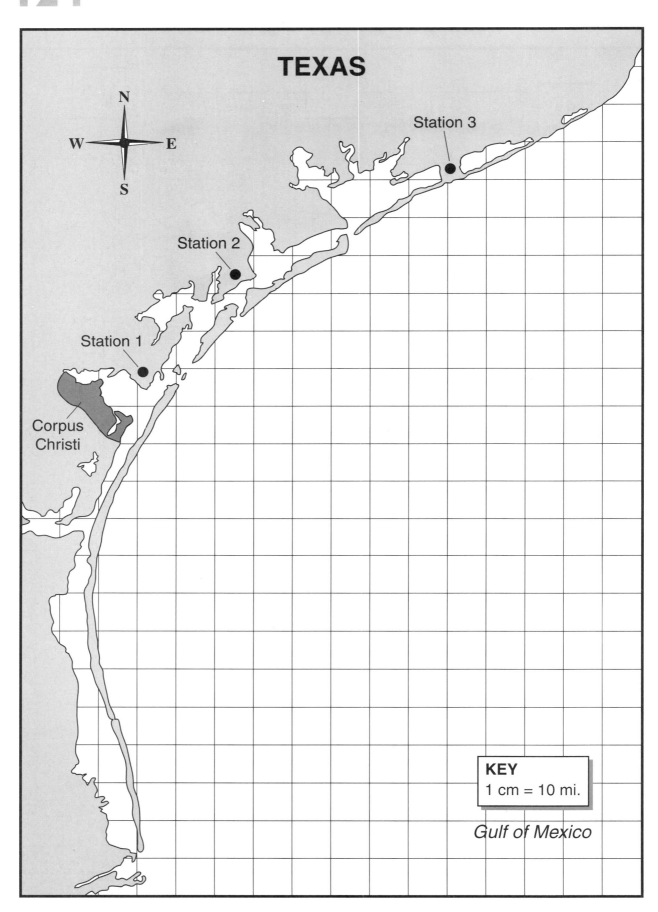

TEXAS

N
W   E
S

Station 3

Station 2

Station 1

Corpus
Christi

KEY
1 cm = 10 mi.

Gulf of Mexico

	1920	1930	1940	1950	1960	1970	1980	1990
New York City	5,620,048	6,930,446	7,454,995	7,891,957	7,781,984	7,894,862	7,071,639	7,322,564
Chicago	2,701,705	3,376,438	3,396,808	3,620,962	3,550,404	3,366,957	3,005,072	2,783,726
Philadelphia	1,823,779	1,950,961	1,931,334	2,071,605	2,002,512	1,948,609	1,688,210	1,585,577
Los Angeles	576,673	1,238,048	1,504,277	1,970,358	2,479,015	2,816,061	2,966,850	3,485,398
Milwaukee	457,147	578,249	587,472	637,392	741,324	717,099	636,212	628,088
Cincinnati	401,247	451,160	455,610	503,998	502,550	452,524	385,457	364,040
Seattle	315,312	365,583	368,302	467,591	557,087	530,831	493,846	516,259
Denver	256,491	287,861	322,412	415,786	493,887	514,678	492,365	467,610
Atlanta	200,616	270,366	302,288	331,314	487,455	496,973	425,022	394,017
Houston	138,276	292,352	384,514	596,163	938,219	1,232,802	1,595,138	1,630,553
Jacksonville	91,558	129,549	173,065	204,517	201,030	528,865	540,920	635,230

Source: www.census.gov